THE BEAUTY HUNTERS

On African Poetry
Series editor: Matthew Shenoda

EDITORIAL BOARD
Matthew Shenoda, Brown University
Kwame Dawes, University of Nebraska–Lincoln
Tjawangwa Dema, Independent scholar/artist
Tsitsi Jaji, Duke University
Mukoma Wa Ngugi, Cornell University
Helen Yitah, University of Ghana

The Beauty Hunters

Sudanese Bedouin Poetry, Evolution and Impact

Adil Babikir

UNIVERSITY OF NEBRASKA PRESS
LINCOLN

The University of Nebraska Press is part of a land-grant institution with campuses and programs on the past, present, and future homelands of the Pawnee, Ponca, Otoe-Missouria, Omaha, Dakota, Lakota, Kaw, Cheyenne, and Arapaho Peoples, as well as those of the relocated Ho-Chunk, Sac and Fox, and Iowa Peoples.

The On African Poetry series is operated by the African Poetry Book Fund. The APBF was established in 2012 with initial support from philanthropists Laura and Robert F. X. Sillerman. The founding director of the African Poetry Book Fund is Kwame Dawes, Holmes University Professor and Glenna Luschei Editor of *Prairie Schooner*.

Library of Congress Cataloging-in-Publication Data
Names: Babikir, Adil, author.
Title: The beauty hunters : Sudanese Bedouin poetry, evolution and impact / Adil Babikir.
Other titles: On African poetry.
Description: Lincoln : University of Nebraska Press, 2023. | Series: On African poetry | Includes bibliographical references and index.
Identifiers: LCCN 2022048759
ISBN 9781496234094 (hardback)
ISBN 9781496235206 (paperback)
ISBN 9781496235503 (epub)
ISBN 9781496235510 (pdf)
Subjects: LCSH: Ḥārdallū, Muḥammad Aḥmad ʻAwaḍ al-Karīm Abū Sin, 1830–1916. | Arabic poetry—Sudan—History and criticism. | Arabic poetry—Bedouin authors—History and criticism. | Aesthetics in literature. |
BISAC: LITERARY CRITICISM / African |
LITERARY CRITICISM / Poetry
Classification: LCC PJ8310 .B233 2023 |
DDC 892.71009892720624—dc23
LC record available at https://lccn.loc.gov/2022048759

Set and designed in Adobe Text by N. Putens.

To the memory of the late Muḥammad Ṭāha al-Gaddāl, a poetry legend who carved his own revolutionary brand of folk poetry.

And to the memory of my late uncle Siddīq wad al-ʾUmda—a poet, singer, and Bedouin poetry lover, whose ecstatic chanting of Bedouin dobait had captivated me as a little boy and must have been one of the earliest influences that lured me into this beautiful world. His memory is still fresh in my mind: a lean figure in Bedouin attire affectionately holding onto a homemade pipe like an Indian snake charmer—and a ceaseless outpouring of emotional songs.

This imagery is as captivating as a painting by an Italian Renaissance artist. A peaceful parade into the bush, an alarm signal and panic, and then the tragedy engulfs the whole scene—and a whole world falls apart!

—TAYEB SALIH

Contents

Acknowledgments ix

Notes on Transliteration xi

Introduction: A Life's Journey in Search of Beauty 1

1. Al-Ḥārdallo's Time 11

2. Romance 18

3. The Nature Lover 38

4. Al-Ḥārdallo's Style 45

5. The Musdār: A Historical Context 55

6. Musdār al-Nijūm: A Journey across the Stars 62

7. Musdār Rufā'a: A Terrestrial Journey across the Buṭāna 69

8. The Role of Bedouin Poetry in Shaping Sudan's Aesthetic Taste 76

9. The Bedouin Poem: A Living Legacy 82

10. The Musdār and the Ḥaqība 90

11. Contemporary Musdārs 94

12. Al-Ḥārdallo's Poems 107

Musdār al-Ṣayd 107

Miscellaneous Quatrains 120

Nostalgia 120

Romance 121

Heartbreak 123

The Ordeal 127

Farewell 128

Arabic Glossary of Local Terms 129

Notes 133

Bibliography 139

Index 141

Acknowledgments

Without the elucidating remarks of the late Dr. Ibrāhīm al-Ḥārdallo, I would not have been able to understand, let alone translate, the work of this great poet. Dr. al-Ḥārdallo's book *Diwan al-Ḥārdallo* (Al-Ḥārdallo's poetry collection) is one of the most authoritative references to the work of this poet. As both a professor of Arabic literature and a grandson of the poet, Dr. al-Ḥārdallo was uniquely positioned to offer not only a reliable biographical account of the life and poetry of his grandfather but also credible explanations of some of the most subtle references in that poetry. That insider's view was also vital for verifying the authenticity of the poems, given that they were communicated only orally across generations and geographies.

I am also thankful to Professor Aḥmad 'Abd al-Rahim Nasr and Professor Sayed H. Hureiz, who read early versions of the manuscript and shared insightful feedback. I found Professor Nasr's exhaustive comments quite useful, and I benefited immensely from Professor Hureiz's extensive study of the musdār as an art form. I drew heavily on his introduction to that book in writing a historical context for the musdār and in discussing two types of the musdār in chapters 6 and 7. Professor Hureiz's book helped me understand the local context of this genre and prepared me for appreciating the verse of this great poet.

Al-Mubārak Ibrāhīm and 'Abd al-Majīd 'Ābdīn's book *al-Ḥārdallo, Shā'ir al-Buṭāna* (Al-Ḥārdallo, the poet of Buṭāna) was helpful in comparing their interpretation of the poems with that of Dr. Ibrāhīm al-Ḥārdallo's. I also found in their book additional quatrains and biographical information that proved quite helpful.

Many other references were helpful reads, such as Dr. 'Izz al-Din Ismā'īl, *al-Shi'r al-Qawmi fi al-Sūdān* (Sudanese folk poetry), and Ṣalāḥ Dahab's article, "al-Ḥārdallo fi Qaṣidatihi al-Malḥamiyyah Musdār al-Ṣayd" (Al-Ḥārdallo's epic, Musdār al-Ṣayd).

Muḥammad 'Abd al-Qadir al-Ḥārdallo was a great help to me in deciphering some of the subtle references in al-Ḥārdallo's poetry and sharing invaluable biographical and other information.

Most of the reference materials I needed for this book were graciously shared by my friend Dr. al-Ḥaj Salim Musṭafa, the veteran librarian and researcher. His enthusiasm and encouragement throughout the various stages pulled me through, and as one well versed in Sudanese culture, he contributed insightful remarks. Over and above, he took upon himself the exhaustive task of putting together the index and bibliography of this book. And I benefited tremendously from my friend Dr. Murtada al-Ghali's sharp eye for detail, apt remarks, and exhaustive review of the manuscript.

This work benefited greatly from the comments of Aḥmad al-Ṭayif, Samia Kergwel, al-Arkam Karrar, Nizār Mubarak, Faṭima Al Sanousi, among others. And as always, I am thankful to my daughter, Mayada, for her thorough review of the manuscript.

Notes on Transliteration

The transliterations style adopted in this book is that of the *International Journal of Middle East Studies* (IJMES), except for minor adaptations in conformity with the mainstream Sudanese vernacular Arabic.

ء	ʾ	س	s	ل	l
ب	b	ش	sh	م	m
ت	t	ص	ṣ (s)	ن	n
ث	th	ض	ḍ (d)	ه	h
ج	j	ط	ṭ (t)	و	w / ū (u)
ح	ḥ (h)	ظ	ẓ (z)	ي	y / ī (i)
خ	kh	ع	ʿ	ا	ā (a)
د	d	غ	gh	ة	a / at
ذ	dh	ف	f	ال	al / -l-
ر	r	ق	q		
ز	z	ك	k		

For names, I generally followed the pronunciations in classical Arabic, except where they contradicted with Sudanese colloquial, in which case I followed the latter.

Place Names

For the most common place names, the conventional English spelling is used; for example, Khartoum (Kharṭūm), Omdurman (Umm Durmān), Gezira (Jazīra), and Berber (Barbar).

Hyphenation

The only hyphenation that appears is the one for the definite article *al* (ال); for example, al-Ḥārdallo. Spaces between Arabic words are rendered by spaces in the transliteration.

Shadda

A *shadda* (geminaton) is a stress that has the effect of doubling the letter in the transliteration; for example, Muḥammad (مُحَمَّد).

THE BEAUTY HUNTERS

Introduction

A LIFE'S JOURNEY IN SEARCH OF BEAUTY

Like most of those who were born and grew up in post-independence Khartoum, my first encounter with Sudanese Bedouin poetry was through the renowned Sudanese musician and singer ʻAbd al-Karīm al-Kābli. Successive generations of city dwellers were fascinated by the stanzas that al-Kābli translated into melodies, either as standalone pieces or as preludes to his popular songs. The presence of many unfamiliar words in those poems failed to prevent the urban population from appreciating their exotic imagery and the unrestrained depiction of emotions.

A huge credit is due to al-Kābli for uncovering the treasures of Bedouin poems and endearing them to the urban population. One of the pieces he put to music was by Muḥammad Aḥmad ʻAwad al-Karim, better known as al-Ḥārdallo, who is the doyen of this art form. It depicts a lover in pain of parting, recalling images of his sweetheart as she steps onto the dancing stage:

From a young age, my heart readily fell in girls' snares.
My passion has now grown cureless.
A gentle hold on her pliant pinkie, she goes breathless,
twisting like a supple branch on the mouth of a watercourse.
Swaying in rhythm with excited beats on the little *shatam* drum,
her exposed beauty to the stars above lending gleam.
Her glittering jewelry and dark hair inflaming my heart.
Your protection, O Lord, from a passion running deep in my bloodstream.

قلبي ألمِن نشوهو للبنات هوّاى
داب من زاد علىّ وغلب الداواى

من مسكة خنيصرو الملو شديد لاواى
بتفهق برا الكبد الحُقن ناواى
خلفولا الشتيم شاشايها جاى جاي
جات بتشلعو الفوقو النجيم ضواى
سِت تِبْرى اب نقِش والداير البارای
يا ستّار علىّ مِنْ غَيّها السرّاى

In another popular prelude to a song, al-Kābli relays a message from al-Ḥārdallo to his brother ʿIbdillah, explaining why he could not catch up with them for Eid celebrations.[1]

Among her age or older, she's peerless.
If ʿIbdillah and the folks could see her,
and the necklace over her ample chest dangling,
they'd excuse my absence from their Eid gathering.

الزول السمح فات الكبار والقدرو
كان شافوهو ناس عِبْدِالله كانوا يعذروا
السبب الحماني العيد هناك أحضرو
درديق الشبيكي البنتو في صدرو

Sudanese Bedouin poetry has different names, depending on the verse structure and the way it is recited. *Murabaʾ* or *marbūʿ* refers to a quatrain composed of four lines. *Namm* or *namim* refers to the act of chanting out the Bedouin verse. This act often takes place in relaxed settings where people gather around an actor who is endowed with a beautiful voice and good singing skills. Some poets chant their own verse, but more often than not, there are popular actors who play that role. Those actors served as custodians of this art form particularly during the early times when oral communication was the only means of preserving it. *Ghuna*, Arabic for "singing," is a term used by the Bedouins to refer to both the act of chanting the verse and to the genre of poetry.

The two broad terms used to refer to Bedouin poetry as a genre are *dobait* and *dobay*. The word *dobay* (دوباي) is derived from the verb *doba* (دوبى) in the past tense, *yadoubi* (يدوبي) in the present tense, which means "to chant."

As a noun, it also means "longing." It is used extensively in both senses in Bedouin poetry.

There is some disagreement about the origin of the word *dobait* in the Sudanese context. Dr. 'Abdul Majid 'Ābdīn maintains that it is a Persian word, *du*, meaning two lines (each containing two parts, which make a four-part quatrain). He also believes that the Sudanese dobait is composed in the *rajaz* meter, that is, a combination of Persian form and Arabian meter. He suggests that before migrating to the Sudan, the Arabian tribes (Rabi'ah, for instance) had been in contact with Persia and must have assimilated that form and eventually brought it along to their new home.[2]

However, many scholars deny the existence of such Persian influence in Sudanese Bedouin poetry. According to Muḥammad al-Wāthiq, the Persian dobait was born six centuries after Islam, yet the Arabian tribes had settled in the Sudan well before the advent of Islam.[3]

Although the term dobait eventually gained prominence in academic circles and urban communities, it is hardly known among the Bedouins. An important finding of al-Ṭayyib Muḥammad al-Ṭayyib's extensive field research is that the word *dobait* is "not heard of" among the Bedouin communities across the Sudan.[4] The universally used term in these communities is *dobay*, in addition to *ghuna, muraba', marbū'*, *namm*, and *namim*, as explained above. The confusion may have to do with the phonological similarity between *dobay* and *dobait*; although neither one is found in the Arabic lexicon. Al-Tayyib believes that *dobay* entered the Sudanese Bedouin glossary from the Beja region of eastern Sudan. "The word does not sound like Arabic, so how come it became part of the jargon of the Arabic-speaking population of central Sudan? Most likely the Arabian tribes that entered the Sudan through the Red Sea and the eastern desert intermingled with the Beja tribes and acquired it from them."[5] This opinion is substantiated by the presence of many Beja words in Buṭāna poetry. The words *shambani*, *fadag*, and *ayatib* are but a few examples. Describing his longing for Um Na'im, al-Ḥārdallo describes his pain as one whose heart is pierced by a sharp arrow.

Go ahead, friends; tell everyone
if I didn't get any better by the evening,

I'll probably die before the morning.
Um Na'im's *shambani* hit me in the heart;
went two-span deep.

ودّوا اخباري يا عُوّادي
قولو مقيلو إن أمسابو بصبح قاضي
شمباني ام نعيم ضارباني بي في فؤادي
قَبلُو مِعَضَّه وشبرين مرق بي غادي

Another example is *ayataib* (أياتيب) meaning "kindness." In another marbū', al-Ḥārdallo seems so resigned to his sweetheart's "war" against him that he prefers it to the kindness of anyone else! حربو معاي أفضل من أياتيب غيرو

The influence of the Beja in Bedouin poetry extended to the numeral system. The Buṭāna poetry carried many references to Beja numerals. Abu Digaina, an eighteenth-century poet describes the Prophet as a full moon that dwarfs everything else. He says:

You are a moon of ten plus a *fadag*,[6]

قمر عشرة وفدق للبالو فيك

Indeed, the efforts of al-Kābli and other folklore researchers and artists, like the late al-Ṭayyib Muḥammad al-Ṭayyib, paved the way for Bedouin poetry to win the attention of a wider audience. However, it was at the beginning of this millennium when it started to gain new ground, thanks to a phenomenal rise in the use of mobile phones and satellite broadcasting. Wide public access to the internet and online platforms enabled traditional forms of Bedouin poetry to spread beyond the Bedouin boundaries and establish a strong presence even in the capital, Khartoum. More interestingly, Bedouin poetry is increasingly finding favor with even the younger generations of both sexes, and the language and cultural barriers that previously held these forms within their original boundaries are now fading away.[7]

The surging popularity of Bedouin poetry is a revival of a centuries-old tradition. Al-Ḥārdallo (1830–1916) is widely seen as one of the most important poets in the Sudan's history. More than a century after his death, he lives on in memory and in song. His verse continues to resonate across generations despite its esoteric Bedouin parlance, thanks perhaps to its rich lyricism and vividly cinematic imagery. Many of his works were set to popular music that can still be heard today in various parts of the Sudan. His romance and nature poetry evokes comparison with such great poets as Imru' al-Qays and Dhul-Rumma, from classical Arabic periods, and the pioneering English Romantic poets, namely, William Wordsworth, Samuel Taylor Coleridge, and John Keats.

Al-Ḥārdallo was born to a wealthy and influential family. His father was the chieftain of the Shukriyah, one of the main nomadic tribes that inhabited the Buṭāna plains, a 120,000-square-kilometer area running from the Ethiopian border across southeastern and central Sudan. Those Bedouins spend a good part of the year on the move in pursuit of grazing areas from the Blue Nile in the west to River Setit in the east, and from Gedaref in the southeast to the northeastern limits of Khartoum.

The nomadic lifestyle has earned the Shukriyah an unquenchable yearning for their abodes and great poetic talents. No wonder their region has long been associated with superb Bedouin verse. Poetry plays a central role in their life and is a form of everyday communication. During their journeys after pasture, at wedding parties and other social events, at battles with other tribes—nearly every aspect of daily life can give birth to beautiful verse that gains currency within the neighborhood and beyond. The most popular themes of their poetry are love, heartbreak, elegy, glorification of knighthood, and praise of nature.

Al-Ḥārdallo owes his fame to a unique combination of factors. Part of his legacy is drawn from his eventful life and its sharp turns, from a well-to-do and carefree life to living penniless in exile away from his birthplace. While his earlier life inspired his love poetry, his later years triggered a different verse bent on nostalgia and a melancholic yearning for the good old days. The musdār, a long poem describing a factual or imaginary journey, is a fascinating narrative full of videographic images of nature in action by a genuine nature-lover and a staunch defender of wildlife. His romance pieces, much larger in number but significantly shorter than the musdārs, show a different side of him: an indulgent, carefree person. Invariably in all themes, however, he produced eloquent and sensational verse that is still broadly quoted all over the country, with some lines of his verse even going around as popular proverbs and aphorisms.

This book sheds light on al-Ḥārdallo's treasured contributions to Bedouin poetry and to Sudanese poetry in general. Delineating his pathbreaking style, the recurrent themes in his poetry, and the sociopolitical influences, will hopefully provide some clues as to how he has become a living legacy.

Another aim of the book is to highlight Sudanese Bedouin poetry as a distinctive art genre and define its role in shaping the Sudan's aesthetic taste and its hybrid cultural identity of the Sudan as an Afro-Arab nation.

Bedouin poetry is deeply rooted in Sudanese culture, dating back to early times when Arab tribes, driven away by drought, migrated out of the Arabian Peninsula and resettled in the pasture-rich plains of Buṭāna in central, eastern, and other parts of the Sudan. The poetry they produced in their new land—although it maintained its original form and some of the main themes—eventually acquired distinct attributes that set it apart as a homegrown art within an African geographical setting.

The unique combination of geographical, political, and sociocultural factors that contributed to the development of Sudanese Bedouin poetry are discussed throughout this book with extensive illustrations from the poetry of al-Ḥārdallo, the most renowned icon of this art form, as well as samples from many of his contemporaries and successors.

The Buṭāna's natural setting has served as the main source of inspiration for the successive generations of Bedouin poets. Rain, in particular, is the most eagerly anticipated event of the year and a trigger of poets' imagination. The advent of the rainy season is a moment of celebration, and it's no wonder it was eternalized in their poetry. Even in his exile away from home, al-Ḥārdallo translates his nostalgia into a live portrait of a whole place coming to life:

> Confirmed news from home: The Buṭāna plains were hit by heavy rain.
> Pouring all night long, it continued unabated into the morning.
> Male crickets raged with lust; udders, even of young cattle,[8] grew full,
> and she-camels enjoyed a lush meal within a short stroll.

الخَبَر اَللكيد قالوا الْبُطانة اتّرَشَّتْ
ساريتنْ تبَقْبِقْ ل الصباح ما انْفَشَّت
هاج فَحَلْ أمْ صِريصر والمانح بشَّتْ
وبت ام ساق على حَدَب الْفريق اتعشَّتْ

Fascination with nature seems to have shaped the Buṭāna poets' perception of beauty. As detailed in chapters 2 and 4, the oryx and the ductile plant are standard benchmarks for women's beauty among Bedouin poets, and, as illustrated in chapters 9 and 10, many metaphors and analogies around this found their way to lyrical and other forms of the sedentary poetry starting from the nineteenth century.

Al-Ḥārdallo's conception of beauty, his attachment to the natural world, and the drastic changes in his life seem to have had a distinctive influence on the content, style, and tone of his verse. An interesting feature of his poetry is that his reference to women's beauty is almost always linked to his celebration of the beauty of nature. Readers of his poetry will not miss his conscious portrayal of women as a salient feature of nature. His praise of a woman's beauty reaches its peak only when it is paralleled to one of nature's elements, particularly the oryxes and the ductile green cane reeds. The same thing happens when the oryx is the focus of his praise. Here, also, human beauty is called upon to complete the picture. Chapter 4 compares al-Ḥārdallo's poems in celebration of nature with the works of the Romantic poets William Wordsworth and John Keats.

Al-Ḥārdallo's poems are composed of either a single marbūʿ or a combination of those units. The former constitutes the vast majority of his verse and addresses broadly diverse topics.

The opening chapter delves into the poet's background, his birthplace, and his influential family's history. It traces his youth and audacious romantic entanglements, on to his adulthood and eventual fall into poverty. This chapter glances at the sociopolitical climate that impacted al-Ḥārdallo's life and resonated in his poetry.

The second chapter deals with al-Ḥārdallo's romance poems, which show a mischievous side to him. It cites poems that describe his many romantic involvements, and it is interesting to note that the underlying theme of his romance poetry is the pain of parting. The chapter also draws comparisons with two great Arab poets, Imru' al-Qays and Dhul-Rumma, as well as with the two most famous Arab love poets, Qays and Jamīl from the Umayyad period.

Few other poets have so wholly devoted themselves to nature as a theme. One often encounters in al-Ḥārdallo's nature poems intense attachment to, and reverence for, his pastoral surroundings. Chapter 3 includes an extensive review of al-Ḥārdallo's longest and most famous ode, "Musdār al-Ṣayd," an imaginary journey across the Buṭāna wilderness, in the company of his most beloved creature, the oryx. Composed of forty quatrains, each providing an independent scene, this poem is a documentary of the oryxes' yearlong wandering in search of water and pasture. It is a journey across seasons and geographical locations of the Buṭāna plains, full of wondrous flora and fauna, but it is also the poet's personal journey of loss and redemption. These scenes are skillfully threaded together into a grand love story with nature.

Chapter 5 provides a historical context by tracing the evolution of the musdār as an art form into the present time. Chapters 6 and 7 illustrate two shining examples by second-generation musdār poets 'Abdallah Ḥamad Wad Shawrāni and Aḥmad 'Awad al-Karīm Abu-Sin.

Chapter 8 traces the impact of Buṭāna poetry on the development of what Muḥammad al-Wāthiq calls a unique Sudanese "aesthetic taste," while chapters 9 and 10 look into the influence of Bedouin poetry in the evolution of lyric poetry in the Sudan starting in the 1920s, with the so-called *ḥaqība*, a unique genre of lyric poetry that set the foundation for the modern Sudanese song. The journey as a theme, exemplified by the musdār, continued to inspire successive generations of poets who took it to new levels. An interesting example, cited in chapter 11, is by Muḥammad Ṭāha al-Gaddāl, who took the musdār beyond the Sudan's boundaries, staging a protest parade to the Statute of Liberty!

Chapter 12 contains translations from al-Ḥārdallo's repertoire of poems, beginning with the long epic "Musdār al-Ṣayd" (160 lines), followed by the quatrains, which are arranged under the following themes: nostalgia, romance, heartbreak, the ordeal, and farewell. The original Arabic text follows in the same order.

In his wandering across the Buṭāna wilderness, in his adventures with women, and in the ups and downs of his life, al-Ḥārdallo lived through a series of journeys in pursuit of beauty, a journey well-documented by superb verse.

One last note about my experience with translating Bedouin poetry: Given the exotic nature of this poetry, I opted for a more liberal approach to translating it, focusing on rendering the poetics and cultural meaning of the verse, which meant that the translated lines sometimes outnumbered the original text. I hope this attempt will help convey some of the treasures of this uniquely Sudanese art form.

1 Al-Ḥārdallo's Time

Al-Ḥārdallo was born in 1830 in Reira, in southeastern Sudan, to a wealthy and influential family.[1] His father, Aḥmad Abu-Sin, was the head of the Shukriyah tribe, which enjoyed a prominent status during the Turkish rule. Aḥmad was named chief sheikh, in which capacity he was in charge of all the tribes dwelling in the area between the White Nile and the borders with Ethiopia. He was also the first Sudanese commissioner of Khartoum, a position he held roughly between 1860 and 1870.[2]

During his youth and a good part of his adulthood, al-Ḥārdallo led a carefree life. His poetry is replete with anecdotes of his affairs with scores of women. This may sound out of line to contemporary readers when judged by present-day standards. However, reading it within its historical context will show that it was a condoned practice within tribal communities at the time.

As illustrated across the book, al-Ḥārdallo was one of the pioneers of Bedouin poetry who played a trailblazing role in the evolution of Sudanese poetry and lyrics and in forming a unique taste for poetry and beauty. From this perspective, and also given its high aesthetic value and unique style, al-Ḥārdallo's love poetry is worth highlighting.

Many Bedouin poems were produced at private gatherings where friends would meet for entertainment and spend the night reminiscing about happy times in the past. Those relaxed settings often gave birth to interactive poems, with the poets in attendance contributing quatrains in turns. Light by their nature, these poems are part of the entertainment atmosphere of those friendly settings and may not bear comparison, in terms of quality, with al-Ḥārdallo's masterpieces. However, they shed light on life in Buṭāna at the time and offer an indispensable source of information about the evolution of Bedouin poetry.

Al-Ḥārdallo made frequent references to his inner circle of friends, namely his brother and fellow poet 'Abdallha. In the introduction I mentioned one piece in which the poet apologized to his other brother 'Ibdillah for his absence from their usual get-together. Quatrains produced in these casual settings reflect a poet full of life, in a cheerful mood.

"Musdār al-Mitairig" was one of the interactive poems produced during those private settings. A *mitairig* is a thin cane carried by men as an ornament and an indication of status and is also used by speakers and poets as part of their body language, to emphasize a point or help create the desired impact on listeners.[3] The subject of this musdār was al-Ḥārdallo's *mitairig*, which mysteriously went missing and turned out to have been taken by none other than the poet's sweetheart! As the story goes, she was supposed to come to his place one night. His guests that particular night stayed longer than usual, and when she did come al-Ḥārdallo had already lost himself to slumber, so she took away his cane as proof that she fulfilled her promise. Missing his cane in the morning, al-Ḥārdallo thought some burglar stole it, but it was 'Abdallah's guess that was proven right. So the whole poem revolves about this.

In the latter part of his life, al-Ḥārdallo and his tribe experienced a cruel downturn with the rise of the Mahdist rule (1885–98). This religious and political movement was launched in 1881 by Muḥammad Aḥmad al-Mahdi against the Khedivate of Egypt, which had ruled the Sudan since 1821. Although the Shukriyah had managed for decades to stay clear of tribal feuds, they antagonized al-Mahdi's successor, Calipha 'Abdullahi, when they sided with a rival faction, al-Ashraf, following al-Mahdi's death.[4] Calipha 'Abdullahi imprisoned many of the Shukriyah leaders, who lost a good part of their wealth and influence and had to take refuge in the Ethiopian borders, particularly following a strong drought that hit Buṭāna in 1889.[5]

The ordeal of the Shukriyah in the hands of the Mahdists is well documented in many historical references as well as in al-Ḥārdallo's verse, which carries frequent references to prominent families of the tribe, such as "the sons of Ḥamad" and "'Amāra and his cousins" who ended up as refugees in Ethiopia.

Even the sons of Ḥamad, once the resort for everyone in need,
have now left, crossed the Atbarawi River to Abyssinia.
Their women with thick hair in oil soaked
are in tears for leaving Reira and their company behind.[6]

رحلوا أولادْ حَمَدْ ألْ للبلَد رُكّازَه
قَطَعوا الأتْبَراوي منوّيين بالبازه
ستات اللَكيك ألْ عقْلَتِنْ نزّازه
بِبْكّن بالدموع لى ريره لى من حازَه

The poet does not forget to describe his personal feelings over this plight.

Today I feel like one who went on a no-return trip,
or one whose arrow went too wide.
Like braids of hair swinging in a woman's neck,
our fate is swinging in the hands of our Creator,
who alone can decide when to take our souls back.[7]

الليله علَيْ مِثْل ألْ خَتَرْ ما عاد
والليله علَيْ مِثْل أل زَرَقْ ما صَاد
اليوم يا امْ وَريدنْ نفّض اللُباّد
ترى الراس بقْطعُه الخالِق مِتين ماراد

Moved by the sight of the once dignified women of the tribe wandering the streets of local towns in torn clothes, he sends this outcry to his brother ʿAbdallah Abu-Sin, lamenting the death of a great figure of the tribe.

Look around, ʿAbdallah;
You will see young oryxes,
tottering around in rags.
What a grieving loss is ab-Sa'ad, folks.[8]

يا عبد الله خوي أنظر قَدُر ما كان
ما شُفْتَ البَهيم الصيد جَنَى الجِذْيان
دجّنْ بلَّرِضْ كسُّوهِنْ الدُلْقانْ
واوجعي الشديد رَقَدْ أبْ سَعَدْ ياخوانْ

Referring to the Matamma incident, when soldiers of Calipha ʿAbdullahi reportedly staged a massacre on the stronghold town of the Jaʾaliyin tribe in the central north of the Sudan, al-Ḥārdallo looks at the dilemma of the town women who were enslaved and forced to serve as house servants.

Go to the towns, ʿAbdallah, and see for yourself,
the girls of Matamma, their hair disheveled,
water skins on their shoulders—
and instead of hair oil and oily perfumes,
lice rampaging through their heads.[9]

يا عبد الله خوي أغْشَ البنادر شوفِنْ
بَنّوت المتمّه اجّدَلَنْ صَفُّوفِنْ
شايلات القِرَبْ والسعون في كتوفِنْ
وبعد خُمْرَه ودِهان سال القَمُلْ برْفُوفِنْ

Al-Ḥārdallo was not personally immune from persecution. He served a brief term of imprisonment in Omdurman, but he managed to win the heart of Calipha ʿAbdullahi, who took him as a court entertainer but also as a personal servant—carrying Calipha's ablution jug and prayer rug and walking behind his horse. That decline in status had a profound effect on al-Ḥārdallo's soul and tainted his poetry with thick shades of bitterness. However, in a bid to protect his tribe from the Calipha's strong hand, al-Ḥārdallo had to use his talent as a poet in stroking the man's ego. Taking advantage of a failed attempt on the Calipha's life, al-Ḥārdallo said:

You have a huge army of loyal men.
When they mount, like greenery they fill the horizon.
Surely short-sighted and unintelligent
who think a bird trap can catch an elephant.[10]

أنصارك كُتار تامينْ عَبِرْة الكيل
زي نبْتَ الرُبَى وكْتين ركوب الخيلْ
كان ماجور زمان وناسَنْ بصَرْها قليلْ
شَرَكْ امْ قيردون كيفِنْ بِقُبْض الفيل

He also had to use his eloquence to save the life of Sheikh ʿAmāra Abu Sin, a key figure in the Shukriyah tribe who had been sentenced to death by Calipha ʿAbdullahi. Addressing the Calipha, al-Ḥārdallo made a fervent appeal for clemency.

Since early adulthood, he was a standout;
always on the backs of battle horses.
O Caliph of the Mahdi, I implore you to forgive ʿAmāra;
here he's standing before you, like a sacrificial lamb.[11]

مِنْ قومت الجهل ولداً مِمّيِّزْ عُومه
حافلات اللُّبُوس فيهِنْ بِغَزِّرْ كومه
خليفتَ المنتَظرْ عماره أغَفِرْ لُومه
جاك كبش الضحيّه الليله آخر يومه

When the Calipha finally pardoned ʿAmāra, one of those present asked al-Ḥārdallo what was so special about ʿAmāra that earned him all that lofty praise. Al-Ḥārdallo's answer was this:

He gives without measure though he never brags about it.
Formidable like a venomous spotted snake.
Intimidating like a lion blocking access to River Setit.
A fierce fighter in battle, yet hospitable at home.[12]

إن ادّاك وكتّر ما بقول أدّيت
أبْ دَرَقْ الموَشّحْ كُلُّو بالسوميت
أبْ رِسْوه أل بِكُرْ حَجَّر وُرودْ سيتيت
كاتال في الخلا وعقبان كريم في البيتْ

Later, Calipha ʿAbdullahi sent al-Ḥārdallo to work as an assistant to his representative at the southeastern part of the country. Apparently the man, known as Wad al-Baṣīr, gave al-Ḥārdallo a hard time and forced him to do the laborious work of loading camels with sorghum sacks and dispatching them to different locations across the eastern borders. That ill-treatment gave rise to bitter remarks.

The Mahdi, for one, was a man worthy of respect.
Now even Wad al-Başīr has squeezed us into a goose asshole.[13]

Echoes of this melancholy mood dominated most of his poetry composed in the last two decades of his life. It was during that tough period in exile that he let out his famous nostalgic outcry.

On a palm frond bed and a straw mat, I had a sleepless night.
My shed hardly offering any shield from cold and rain.
Kept awake by memories of her sweet coquettish whisper till dawn,
I couldn't get up in time to load sorghum on camel backs.[14]

البارِحْ رُقادي كَسيدة فوقَه بْريش
راكوبةً تجيبْ صَقْطة وْمعاها رّشيشْ
اللحماني ما اشهّل جُمال العيشْ
هُنْهيناً بِسوّنّو الدّغش بي شيشْ

That mood reached its peak a few years before his death when he lost all his property and had to sell his own sword. In the lines below he laments how from a proud owner of a huge herd of cattle, he plunged to pennilessness. The third and fourth lines became a popular proverb.

Gone is my herd of cattle that'd suck many wells dry.
Today for handfuls of sorghum I sold ab-Nāmah, my cherished sword.
Truly, life can be tame enough to be led by a spider's thread.
But can also be stubborn enough to break free from steel reins.[15]

بعد اَمْ بوح تقطّعْ جامَت العداد
بِعْت اب نامه بي قِيمَتْ عَشَرتْ امداد
إنْ جادتْ بي خيت العنكبوت تِنْقاد
وان عاقتْ تقطّع سِلسِل الحدّاد

Like a skillful theater director, he chooses a closing scene that drives the tragedy to its climax. Employing local myth, he draws an emotional picture of his impending death, with a camel parade descending from heaven and parking on the horizon waiting for the moment when his soul leaves his body to take it to heaven. He closes that scene with an outcry against a world that has lost "nobleness and modesty" but also with an emotional farewell shout-out to his beloved land.

The heavenly camels have arrived,
like a flock of pigeons lined up on the horizon.
Time to leave a world from which, alas, nobleness and modesty are gone.
But I'll always miss my beloved valley, ever bountiful and green.[16]

زُمْل القدرة جَنْ وفي الوَطا ما خَتّنْ
طارن لى السماء وْمِتْل القماري اسّتّنْ
الجُود والحَياَ منّ العِقول انختَّنْ
طال الشوق على الوادي ابْ عِيوشَنْ شتّنْ

Just as it echoed the dramatic turns in the poet's personal life, al-Ḥārdallo's poetry carried glimpses of the sociopolitical developments in the Sudan during his lifetime, having lived through three distinct eras: the Turco-Egyptian rule (1820–85), the Mahdist rule (1885–98), and part of the Anglo-Egyptian era (1898–1956). While each one of these eras left a distinct mark on his poetry, their combined impact contributed significantly to the richness of his experience and helped establish him as one of the most prominent cultural icons in the Sudan.

2 Romance

Al-Ḥārdallo's romantic poems have gone viral across the Buṭāna and the country at large since they were composed in the early twentieth century. Passing orally from one generation to another, some of them were adapted into popular songs. As mentioned in the introduction, many of al-Ḥārdallo's short pieces were popularized by Sudanese singer and musician 'Abd al-Karīm al-Kābli.

The example below is a powerful and lively depiction of a woman on the dancing stage; so delicate she can't endure a gentle hold on her little finger and so beautiful she lends gleam to the stars! Apart from the fascinating deployment of simile and metaphor, the piece offers a moving image of a woman whose beauty moved the drum beater to speed up the tempo!

From a young age, my heart readily fell in girls' snares.
My passion has now grown cureless.
A gentle hold on her pliant pinkie, she goes breathless,
twisting like a supple branch on the mouth of a watercourse.
Swaying in rhythm with excited beats on the little *shatam* drum,
her exposed beauty to the stars above lending gleam.
Her glittering jewelry and dark hair inflaming my heart.
Your protection, O Lord, from a passion running deep in my bloodstream.

قلبي ألمِن نشوهو للبنات هوّاى
داب من زاد عليّ وغلب الداواى
من مسكة خنيصرو الـمو شديد لاواى
بتفهق برا الكبد الحُقن ناواى

خلفولا الشتيم شاشايها جاى جاي
جات بتشلعو الفوقو النجيم ضواى
سِت تِبْرى اب نقِش والداير البارای
يا ستّار عليَّ مِنْ غَيّها السرَّاى

Another piece, also set to music by al-Kābli, features a young oryx strolling around, her beauty flames sparing no one. Here, also, the symbolic reference is discernible.

Strolling around, her hair reaching down to her waist,
she reminds me of a young oryx who's taken
Mount Wad Ḥārir as her grazing zone
At close range or far past, from her flames no one is immune.

رايهوبةً على قوز ود حرير مسدارك
تاقى المشيه قودى الحزمك لا قصارك
حسس الغادى منك وا أذى الفى جوارك
والله يكافى محنك يا المتلعبة نارك

Sudanese singer and musician Muḥammad al-Amīn enraptures his fans with this piece from al-Ḥārdallo.

O creator of the universe
I have been holding a big secret deep in my heart,
unwilling to share it except with one who can appreciate it.
The young oryx at the heart of the green valley,
has been playing havoc with my heart, folding and unfolding it.

يا خالق الوجود أنا قلبي كاتِمْ سِرُّو
ما لقيت مِنْ يدرِك المَعْنى بيهو أبِرُّو
بَهَمَتْ مَنْصَح الوادي المِخَدَّرْ دِرُّو
قَعَدَتْ قلبي تطوي وكل ساعه تفِرّو

The novel imagery and outpouring lyricism have won al-Ḥārdallo the hearts of poetry lovers of all generations. His skillful employment of metaphor lends vigor and freshness to his images.

Last night I was with her,
soft and green as a cane on a watercourse.
We were chatting and laughing, and hours flew by.
Until ostriches fell off horsebacks
in the race to the sky's exit gate,
she was not responsive enough,
but was not entirely tough.

البارِحْ أنا وقَصَبة مَدَالق السيل
في ونسة وْبَسِطْ لامِنْ قَسَمنا الليل
وقْتين النّعام اشّقْلَبَن بُو الْخيل
لا جادتْ ولا بِخْلَتْ علَي بالْحيل

Ostriches and horses refer to star formations created by the imaginative power of the Bedouins. At the late hours of the night, the stars seem to form what looks like ostriches falling off horsebacks. To the Bedouins, the sight of such constellations is a sign of imminent dawn break.

The above snapshot by al-Ḥārdallo calls to memory the great pre-Islamic poet Imru' al-Qays (501–44), who was also carefree and had thrilling adventures with women. In the following piece from his famous *mu'allaqa*, he relates a sensual moment with 'Unaizah.

On that day I entered the howdah, the camel's howdah of 'Unaizah!
And she protested, saying, "Woe to you, you will force me to travel on foot."
She repulsed me, while the howdah was swaying with us.
She said, "You are galling my camel, Oh Imru' al-Qays, so dismount."
Then I said, "Drive him on! Let his reins go loose, while you turn to me.
Think not of the camel and our weight on him. Let us be happy.
Many a beautiful woman like you, Oh 'Unaizah, have I visited at night;
I have won her thought to me, even from her children have I won her."[1]

ويَوْمَ دَخَلْتُ الخِدْرَ خِدْرَ عُنَيْزَةٍ
فَقَالَتْ: لَكَ الوَيْلَاتُ!،إنَّكَ مُرْجِلِي
تَقُولُ وقَدْ مَالَ الغَبِيْطُ بِنَا مَعًا:
عَقَرْتَ بَعِيْرِي يَا امْرأَ القَيْسِ فَانْزِلِ

فَقُلْتُ لَهَا: سِيْرِي وأَرْخِي زِمَامَه
ولَا تُبْعِدِيْنِي مِنْ جَنَاكِ المُعَلَّلِ
فَمِثْلِكِ حُبْلَى قَدْ طَرَقْتُ ومُرْضِعٍ
فَأَلْهَيْتُهَا عَنْ ذِي تَمَائِمَ مُحْوِلِ
إِذَا مَا بَكَى مِنْ خَلْفِهَا انْصَرَفَتْ لَهُ
بِشَقٍّ، وتَحْتِي شِقُّهَا لَمْ يُحَوَّلِ

While both al-Ḥārdallo and Imru' al-Qays boast of their ability to win the hearts of women, the latter seems more outspoken in rendering elaborate description of his intimate moments, as shown in the above example. This fits well with the personality of a poet who is keen to present himself as a daring person who heeds no bounds when it comes to women. Although al-Ḥārdallo is no different from Imru' al-Qays in this respect, he elected, in the example cited above, to conceal the identity of his love. He managed to create a highly powerful image by portraying himself in this scene laughing and chatting all night long with an anonymous woman who is "not responsive enough, yet not totally tough"!

The imagery of heavenly ostriches falling off horsebacks shares some resemblance with descriptions of stars as seen in the poetry of renowned Arab poets such as Dhul Rumma (696–735).

And I threw a glance at the stars as if I were in the saddle a hungry noble vulture—
Whilst the constellation of Gemini had inclined to setting until it was like
a herd of wild cows suspended upon a sandy hillock opposite.[2]

وَأَرمي بِعَينَيَّ النُجومَ كَأَنَّني
عَلى الرَحل طاوٍ مِن عِتاقِ الأَجادِل
وَقَد مالَتِ الجَوزاءُ حَتّى كَأَنّها
صِوارٌ تَدَلّى مِن أَميلٍ مُقابِلِ

Al-Ḥārdallo's eloquence, physical attractiveness, and social standing endeared him to women, and as his poetry shows, he did not seem to have any self-restraint. Although he had been involved in numerous affairs with women, the underlying theme of his romance poetry was the pain of parting.

This theme predominated his late poetry, most of which was composed in exile, away from Buṭāna.

Great news from Aḥmad;
The valley is full to the brim, he said.
I can't see why we should here stay,
with no money to spend,
or a soulmate to drive boredom away.

الخَبَر اللَكيد الليلة أحمد جابو
قال الوادي سال واتْقَرّنَنْ تبّابه
إن سَعَلونا نِحْنَ قْعادنا شِنْ أسبابه
لا مصروف ولا زولَنْ بِنِتْسَلابه

The prevalence of the heartbreak theme in al-Ḥārdallo's poetry does not sit well with a man who is known to have been exceptionally skillful in winning the hearts of females. Unlike such famous Arab love poets as Qays and Jamīl, who eternalized their love for their soul mates Layla and Buthaynah, al-Ḥārdallo seemed more open to sharing his heart with many. Interestingly, he stood out as one who would unreservedly mention the names of his female partners, praising their beauty and sharing private details of his affairs with them. The prevalent practice among his contemporaries and even more recent poets was to allude to the women in their poems by some obscure symbols, like their first initial. In the case of al-Ḥārdallo, I counted at least thirteen female names in his poetry, such as al-Tayah, Zainab, Ḥamdiyah, and Khajījah, besides others he referred to by nicknames such as Um Rishaim (lit., one with a nose ring), Um Na'īm (lit., mother of Na'īm), and Um Girain (lit., the long-haired). Here are examples of his praise for al-Tāyah, whose name appears frequently in his poetry.

In vain I tried to conceal my longing for al-Tayah;
it's turning painful like snakebites.
When I recall her curled hair and glittering earrings.
I realize my passion for [Um Na'im] is as strong as ever.

غَيْ التابة دَسّيتو وأبَى يندسْ
أوّل كان ملاسِعْني وْدحين بانْ بسْ
تِحتَ العُقْلة وقْتْ اتلامع الكَسْگسْ
قدْر النملة مِنْ غَي أم نعيم ما خسْ

It's her smile beaming from afar, like glittering clouds,
that's sent me wandering under the hot sun.
Al-Tayah's beauty is comparable to none,
except mountain-dwelling oryxes.
But to be honest, O ʿAmara, I'm still attracted to al-Sara.

الفِرّه البرا المِزْرَى اب سحابةَ جارّة
شِنْ درّعني العيا ولَفْح السُّواجه الحارّة
شبه (التايه) في شات القَنانه الفارّه
لاكين يا عماره قلبي رايد السارّه

There is another group of unnamed females.

Can't you see where I ended up?
One day unconscious, another an aimless wanderer.
I can't stand my parting from a soft sweetheart,
who bears resemblance to the Basyai oryx.

ما بتشوفني هسّع بقيت مي ياي
يوماً تبْ أغيّبْ ويوم أطشْ بي خلاي
فَرْقْ النية بلحيل قلْ عليّ حياي
فيها شبه خِلَق بُرِّيبة الباسياي

Heartache's put its marks on me, visible to all.
My very life is now at stake.
If I ever get to have a deep inhale from her armpits,
nothing will ever put us apart again.

غيّها فيّ ظاهر للبدور معرِفْتو
في الباين علي دمّي العزيز انا خفتو

عرقاً في المناكبْ كان كِتِبْ كارفتو
داك لومَكْ علَيْ ما تقول عُقُبْ فارقتو

The theme of nostalgia occupies a prominent place in Bedouin poetry in general, due to their nomadic lifestyle and frequent movement in search of water and green pastures. In the case of al-Ḥārdallo, it also has to do with his restless soul and unfettered pursuit of beauty.

I yearned for the time when I was my own master.
Riding the long distances to reach them [my girlfriends].
To their lips I was expert at finding my way.
That was a time when life was particularly nice to me.

كم شويَمْ لِهنْ وكتاً بفاقِقْ ورَيّس
كمْ ودّيت لِهن من عِندي واحدْ كَيّس
بسْرِقْ دغْمَتِنْ نَعَمِنّي فيهِن سَيِّسْ
دا وكتْ الزمان بِلْحيل مَعانا كويّسْ

The sight of young oryxes playing gaily in the wilderness evokes unrestrained wishes.

Mount Wad Diyab is still inhabited by oryxes.
Their youngsters jubilantly playing around.
Should I with the means endowed,
I would forsake my own home and choose theirs as my abode.

قوزْ ود ضياب يا اللّيل تَرَى بي شْياهو
بَهَماً بِطَرِّدْ فرحان وعاجبو خلاهو
زولاً في ام قدود المولى كان أداهو
بِقْعُدْ عِنْدَهِنْ بِتْرُكْ لَهِنْ ماواهو

This echoes similar sentiments expressed by the great sixth-century poet Zuhayr ibn Abi Sulma. Coming across what he suspected was the abode of his ex-wife, Ummi Awfa, twenty years after their separation, triggered strong emotions.

Does the blackened ruin, situated in the stony ground
between Durraj and Mutathallam, which did not speak to me,
when addressed, belong to the abode of Ummi Awfa?
And is it her dwelling at the two stony meadows,
seeming as though they were the renewed tattoo marks in the sinews of the wrist?
The wild cows and the white deer are wandering about there,
one herd behind the other, while their young are
springing up from every lying-down place.
I stood again near it [the encampment of the tribe of Awfa],
after an absence of twenty, and with some efforts,
I know her abode again after thinking awhile.[3]

أَمِنْ أُمِّ أَوْفَى دِمْنَـةٌ لَمْ تَكَلَّـمِ
بِحَـوْمَانَةِ الـدُّرَّاجِ فَالمُتَثَلَّـمِ
وَدَارٌ لَهَـا بِالرَّقْمَتَيْـنِ كَأَنَّهَـا
مَرَاجِيْعُ وَشْمٍ فِي نَوَاشِرِ مِعْصَـمِ
العِيْنُ وَالأَرْآمُ يَمْشِينَ خِلْفَـةً
وَأَطْلاؤُهَا يَنْهَضْنَ مِنْ كُلِّ مَجْثَمِ
وَقَفْتُ بِهَا مِنْ بَعْدِ عِشْرِينَ حِجَّةً
فَـلأياً عَرَفْتُ الدَّارَ بَعْدَ تَوَهُّـمِ

Al-Ḥārdallo draws melancholic scenes when he is in the throes of homesickness, away from his loved ones. Anguish of separation from his beloved and excess of passion and longing are among the dominant colors of his fascinating pieces of art.

Heavy worries landed on me.
Distracted and distant all day and night;
a gaunt tummy with a bruised heart I turned.
Even solid stones won't stand such pain.
Yet I never lose hope in the Lord's blessing.

كَبَس الْهَمْ عليْ ليلي ونهاري مْسرّحْ
بطني اشّيمَطَتْ قلبي البِفِر مِجّرّح
الصايدني كان صاد الحُجار بِتْمرّح
لكنْ رحمة المولى الوسيعة تْفَرّحْ

On a palm frond bed and a straw mat, I spent a sleepless night.
My shed hardly offering any shield from cold and rain.
Kept awake by memories of her sweet coquettish whisper till dawn,
I couldn't get up in time to load sorghum on camel backs.

البارِحْ رُقادي گسيدة فوقَه بْريش
راكوبةً تجيبْ صَقْطة وْمعاها رّشيشْ
اللحماني ما اشهّل جُمال العيشْ
هُنْهيناً بِسوّنّو الدّغش بي شيشْ

Repent her love, friends urged me.
But how can I forsake one,
with such a neck, long and proud?
Of me her passion wouldn't let go,
beyond cure, like a mystic lover I grew.
Don't think even Prophet Job as much pain endured.

إتلموا الجماعة وقالوا ليّ تتوب
من العُنقو زيّ الشمعدان مضْبوب
فاتْ فيّ الفوات وبقيتَ زي مجذوبْ
الحاس بيهو ما ظنيتو مسّ ايوبْ

In contrast to this melancholy tone, we see a cheerful person when he is in company. Lyrical praise of beauty takes the center stage.

Last night rumors almost split us apart.
But proven false, the fun did start.
Dancing like a cane on the stream mouth,
the stripes on her cheeks have owned my heart.

البارِخْ حَديسْ الناس بِدُور افْرِقْنا
كُلُّو مرَقْ كِضِبْ عُقْبان صِفينا وْرُقْنا
الدرعة أم شلوخاً سِتةّ مالكة عشُقْنا
تتمايخْ مِتِلْ قَصَبة مَناصح الحُقْنه

He often sends messages of apology to his friends, telling them of the compelling reasons that prevented him from joining them to celebrate festive days. Behind the veil of that apology one can read a teasing tone!

Among her age or older, she's peerless.
If ʿIbdillah and the folks could see her,
and the necklace over her ample chest dangling,
they'd excuse my absence from their Eid gathering.

الزول الصّباه فاتْ الكبار والقدْرو
كان شافوهو ناسْ عبد الله كانوا يعذْروا
السببْ الحماني العيدْ هِناكَ أحَضْروا
دُرْديق الشّبيكي الفصّلو فوقْ سدْرو

Nostalgia is an underlying theme across all genres of Sudanese poetry. Poets of all generations translated their homesickness into heartbreaking verse. In one of his early experiences with life in exile, Ṣalāḥ Aḥmad Ibrāhīm draws an image of a lonely person, "secluded like an Indian outcast" on a festive day when everyone was elegantly dressed.[4]

I remember my mother and brothers,
and he who deep at night,
recites lengthy parts of the Quran.
In my country, the faraway land
where I left behind my best friends;
far beyond the sea and the desert.
In my country, where strangers are warmly welcomed,
and guests favored with the last drop of water,
in the peak of summer;
with children's dinner,
or, when there is little to offer,
with the last portion of boiled beans,
served with warm smiles.

وأنا جوعان
جوعان ولا قلب يأبه
عطشان وضنوا بالشُربه
والنيل بعيد
النيل بعيد
الناس عليهم كل جديد
وأنا وحدى . . .
منكسر الخاطر يوم العيد
تستهزئ بى أنوار الزينة والضوضاء
تستهزئ بى أفكاري المضطربة
وأنا وحدى
فى عزلة منبوذ هندي
أتمثل أمي، اخواني،
والتالي نصف الليل طوال القرآن
فى بلدي
فى بلد أصيحابى النائي
الأعصم خلف البحر وخلف الصحراء
فى بلدي
حيث يعزُ غريب الدار، يُحب الضيف
ويخص بآخر جرعة ماء عز الصيف
بعشا الأطفال
ببليل البشر والإيناس إذا ما رقّ الحال

From the abyss of agony, he calls for help.

Full of grief and pain I started to sing:
O migrating birds to my homeland heading
for God's sake, take me along.
I am surely ready to go.
Fate has torn down my wings.

But the birds took off.
They didn't understand my song!

أسبوع مرّ وأسبوعان
وأخذت أغنى فى شجو، أملى ظاهر
يا طير الهجرة . . . يا طائر
يا طيراً وجهته بلادي
خذني بالله أنا والله على أهبة
قصت أقدار أجنحتي
وأنا فى زاوية أتوسد أمتعتى
ينحسر الظلُّ فأمضى للظل الآخر

لكن الطير مضى عنى
لم يفهم ما كنت أغنى.

Seeking the good offices of birds, and the breeze, is quite common in Sudanese poetry, particularly lyrical verse. In another piece, Ṣalāḥ himself makes another plea to a flock of migrating birds.

Before quenching your thirst,
please stop by a small house.
Through the lit window you'll see
a beautiful girl weaving a hankie
for a soulmate far away.
Stop by her side, kiss her hands, and tell her
I'm still as faithful as ever.

بالله يا طير
قبلما تشرب تمر على بيت صغير
من بابو . . . من شباكو بيلمع ألف نور
تلقى الحبيبة بتشتغل منديل حرير
لحبيب بعيد
أقيف لديها . . . وبوس ايديها . . . وانقل إليها
وفاي ليها . . . وحبي الأكيد.

The case of Muḥammad al-Mahdi al-Majzoub seems to be a chronic one.[5] He is addicted to homesickness! The symptoms started from early childhood when he quickly grew frustrated at the hard chores he had to do at the *khalwa*, the Quranic school, which included daily firewood collection trips. But moving to the capital Khartoum brought little relief to his restless soul, as he felt so estranged from his new environment he yearned for a return to his village in the far north. Reminisces of a wedding parade strolling along the Nile bank reinforced this feeling in him.

> In the heat of *dalluka* drumbeats,[6]
> the young girls were casting charms,
> from kohl-lined eyes,
> where beauty felt at home.
> Tonight, mother of the bride, we brought you
> our cream of the cream;
> palm fronds in our hands,
> a good omen for green times to come.
> Virgins as soft as young plants,
> nursed in the shades for blooming time.
> Rapture flying out of the drums,
> like flocks of birds taking to the sky,
> as the wedding parade gaily slid along the Nile bank.
> We would catch rare glimpses of unguarded beauty,
> yet we never go beyond the limits.

. . . .

البُنيَّاتُ في ضِرام الدلاليك تسـتَّرْنَ فتنةً وانبهار
من عيون تلفَّتَ الكحلُ فيهنَّ وأصغى هُنيهةً ثمّ طارا
نحن جئنا إليك يا أمّها الليلة بالزين والعديل المُنتَّقى
نحن جئناك حاملين جريد النخل فألا على اخضرار ورزقا
العذارى ألوانُهُنَّ الرقيقات نباتُ الظلالِ شفَّ وحارا
رأمَتْه الخدورُ ينتظرُ الموسم حتى يشعّ نورا ونارا
ينبري الطبل ينفض الهزجَ الفينانَ طيرا تفرقا واشتجارا
موكبٌ من مواكب الفرح المختال عصرا
في شاطئ النيل سارا
الجمالُ الغريرُ يسفر غفلانَ فلم ننسَ في الزحام الجوارا
والعبير الحنون هلَّل في صدري طيفا موصلا واعتذارا

نحن جئنا إليك يا أمّها الليلةَ بالزين والعديل المُنقّى
نحن جئناك حاملين جريدَ النخل فألا على اخضرار ورزقا

The cheerful, celebrative mood continues to build.

A proud community servant did the honors;
carrying around the incense burner,
barefooted, in brisk steps, all smiles, he warmly welcomed the parade.
An elated old woman recited warm-hearted verse,
her voice undulating, recalling past glories,
the girls clapping to the rhythm, while shooting glances around;
a mischievous gazelle straightened her dress,
behind others' backs, she showed me her necklace
a pigeon stepped forward, uncovered her hair,
and spread wings and chest,
exposing gleaming scars on the cheeks.
Tonight, mother of the bride, we brought you
a groom who is the cream of the cream;
the best match for a bride,
who is a queen among her maids;
a wellborn. A well-guarded pearl,
whose depths no diver dared to probe.
A broken-hearted sprang high.
A whip thundered on his shoulders as he landed.
He did not flinch, though;
for parting is more painful.
A highbred waiting for her long-awaited knight,
greeted him with a waft of fragrance from her braided hair;
an overt gesture but a short encounter,
and the beauty withdrew from the dancing circle.
With a shy smile,
she quickly took back in,
a mutinous finger that peeked out of her robe,
dusting my glances off her bracelets;
no communication allowed, I was warned.

ومشى بالبخور مَن جعل الخدمة في الحي نخوة وابتدارا
حافيا مسرع الخطى باسم النجدة حيًّا حفاوةً وابتشارا
وعجوز تحمستْ حشدتْ شعرا تعالى حماسة وافتخارا
قلّبت صوتها تأمّل أمجادا قدامى فرقّ حينا وثارا
رفعت فوق منكبٍ طبلَها الصيدح تحت الأكُفّ خفقا
يتغنى لأنفسٍ إن تشهيّنَ طلبنَ الحلال قسما وحقّا
وتشيل البنات صفقا مع الطبل ورمْقا من العيون ورشقا
وغزالٍ مُشاغبٍ أصلح الهدم أراني في غفلةِ النّاس طوقا
تتصدى حمامة كشفت رأسا وزافت بصدرها مستطارا
شلّخوها حتى تضيء فأضمرتْ حنانا لأمها واعتذارا
نحن جئنا إليك يا أمها الليلة بالبحر والعريس المنقى
حجبوها وليّنوا العيش ما كان حجاب الكنين قيدا ورقا
هي ستُّ البنات ستُّ أبيها كرما يحفظ الجوار وصدقا
وجلوها فريدة جفل الغواص عن بحرها خطارا وعمقا
وهوى عاشقٌ وطار وأهوى السوطُ رغْدا بمنكبيه وبرقا
يتحدى عقوبة الصبر فالحرمان أمسى من السياط أشقا
مُهرة "حرة" وتنتظر الفارس يحمى حريمها والذمارا
وأتاهُ العبير من خمل الشبال حيّاه جهرة لا سرارا
موعد لا لقاء فيه وتاجوج تولت عفافة وانتصارا
وبنانٍ توضّحت وطواها الثوب حيا ببسمة تتوارى
نفضتْ عن سوارها بصري يسعى إليها فما تحب الحوارا

At this point the cheerful mood transforms into a desire to escape from "this alien city."

Who would take me back to my playful days?
Who would save me from an exile,
that usurped my soul and lent me a false face?
....
I long for my innocent village,
that knows nothing about my sufferings,
here in this alien city;
alone in a hotel with no neighbors around,
no relatives, or acquaintances;

swallowed in utter darkness;
climbing the rocky nights with a blind lantern;
longing for the deep massage of *dilka*,
the scent of *karkaar*,
and the silky *garmaṣiṣ* gown;
watching the caravans of palm trees,
and the Nile as their escort and singer;
my water jar is full,
Treating myself to cold sips of Nile water,
from an engraved gourd utensil.

لهف نفسي على صباي الذي كان
وما فيه من لعاب العذارى
من عذيري من غربة أخذت روحي
وألقت عليّ وجها مُعارا

آه من قريتي البريئة لا تعلم كم في مدينة الترك أشقى
فندق لا جوار فيه ولا أرحامَ تنهى ولا معارفَ تبقى
وطواني الدُّجى هناك ومصباحي عمى
في صخرة الليل يرقى
أشتهي الدلكة العميقة والكركار والقرمصيص ماج ورقا
وبعيني قوافل النخل والنيل حداها تجيء وسقا فوسقا
بردت جرتي وذا القرع المنقوش يسقى حلاوة النيل طلقا

While in the "alien city," which he actually called "the city of the Turks," he sought another escape route, this time to south Sudan, deeper in continental Africa.

I wish I were among the Negros
My steps swaying to the rhythm of my rabab.
Free to gulp marisa in pubs.
Gobbling freely, to no one's discontent.
Even falling on the street.
My eyes blurred by liquor,
lit up with outrageous rapture;

unrestrained by ancestral nobility claims
of Qurayshis or Tamims.[7]

وليتني في الزنوجِ ولي ربابٌ
تميدُ به خطايَ وتستقيمُ
وأجترعُ المريسةَ في الحواني
وأهذرُ لا ألامَ ولا ألومُ
وأصرعُ في الطريقِ وفي عيوني
ضبابُ السُكر والطربُ الغشومُ
طليقٌ لا تُقيِّدني قريشٌ
بأحسابِ الكرامِ ولا تميمُ

He went even further to claim a hybrid identity.

My veins are endowed with stubbornness from the Negros
even if my verse is endowed with eloquence from the Arabs.[8]

عندي من الزنج أعراق معاندة
وإن تشدق في أشعاري العرب

On account of that claim, al-Majzoub is looked at as a source of inspiration for the Jungle and the Desert group, which probed a third way from the Arabism and Africanism in Sudanese culture.[9] However, critic Abdel Goddous el-Khatim maintains that al-Majzoub's emotional pieces about Africa were driven not by a search for identity but by pure longing for the "innocence of early humanity."[10]

A salient feature of al-Majzoub's poetry, which he shares with al-Ḥārdallo and Bedouin poets in general, is the extensive use of cultural references. The above examples from his poetry contain words such as *dalluka* (a popular drum), *dilka* (a homemade body massage dough), *karkaar* (a homemade hair oil), *garmaṣiṣ* (a silky female bed gown), and *marisa* (locally made sorghum wine). These words, as well as references to the parade to the Nile, a tradition dating back to the ancient Nubian era, the celebrative whipping of young males as part of wedding festivals, and the paraphrasing of a popular wedding song, all add a local flavor to the poem and lend it a unique Sudanese character.[11]

To me, al-Majzoub's poetry lent voice to the call by critic and poet Hamza al-Malik Tambal (1897–1951) for a new literature that is more reflective of the local culture. Tambal's call was an important milestone in the evolution of Sudanese literature as it marked a significant departure from the conventional way of writing poetry, which was fully obsessed with classical Arabic poetry.[12] While Tambal may be credited, along with al-Amīn Ali Madani, with setting the theoretical framework for the new literary current, al-Majzoub can easily be classified among the pioneers who set the course for that current.[13]

The rich repertoire of Bedouin poetry was a main source of inspiration for al-Majzoub. By its very nature, Bedouin poetry reflects the local culture more powerfully than any other art form through intensive use of local idioms and cultural references, portrayal of panoramic views of the natural landscape, and employment of the vernacular as the medium of expression.

Back to al-Ḥārdallo's romance poetry, another interesting feature is that he uses the oryx and the girlfriend interchangeably as his benchmark of beauty. At the peak of his fascination with his love, the image of the oryx invades him. In the following piece, he offers a grand reception for a girl named Jazīrah who settled in his native village of Reira.

My verse is tasteless without a good mention of Gazira.
My village Reira is thrilled to host such a beauty.
Soft thighs and a cushioned breast,
and a necklace like a white streak on a young oryx.

بلاش غنانا الما ذكَّرنا جَزيره
نار بيها البلد واتشرفتْ بَهَا ريره
ليَّن فخدَها المِتْل المَخَدَّة سْديره
فيها شويرة اللدتو أمه محيره

In the following one, al-Tayah is likened to an oryx.

My longing for this young oryx who left Dirrat al-Karrami,
left me a gaunt figure with weak bones.
My passion for cheek-striped[14] al-Tayah gave me sleeplessness.
She has all the beauty features of a young hornless oryx.

من ديفةَ الْ بغادرَنْ دِرّت الكَرّامي
اللحم انْسَلَبْ رابَنْ عليّ عضامي
التاية ام شليخ حسرورها قلّ منامي
فيها مَكَمّلات خِلق الجدي البعّامي

In another snapshot, he likens the oryxes to girls wearing jewelry.

Leaving them in wait at Ḥajar al-Ṣifayyah,
at al-Dahsaraib he found *gombaar* and cucumber vines.
Are these fascinating oryxes any less in charm,
than necks with gold pendants studded?

خلاّهن على حَجر الصِفَيّة خْبوس
ولقى في الدهسريب قُمبار وعِرْقْ فقّوس
في المَخلوقة شِن تشْبه مَعيز امْ روش
غير ال في وَريدِن شولَقِن مرْصوصْ

The white-necked oryx around Ellao al-Ni'am mound often seen,
has shackled my mind to the glittering beads on her hair.
Her spear, naturally sharp, needs no further grinding,
from close range penetrated me.

دَرْعاتاً على عليوّ النَعام مراقه
دَرَجَتْ عقلي في نجيم عُقْلَته أم براقه
تَفْ أم إيد نَفِجْ حَرْبَته مي زرّاقه
حادة برا نَفِخْ فوراً كتير وطراقه

In the following quatrain he draws an interesting analogy between a proud girlfriend who is not responsive enough and a she-camel that produces a scanty amount of milk that cannot quench your thirst.

The likes of Ḥamdiyah never ride on donkey back.
She never gives you a satiating drink.
When in a generous mood, she would only give you a small sip,
leaving you desperate for more.

حمْدية السِرور ما ركّبوك فوقْ عَرْ
ما بتمجِّدك تقْطَعْ قَراك بالمرْ
إن جادتْ عليك تدّيك مِوِيخراً دَرْ
وعُقبان ترْبِعَكْ لامن تضوق الشَرْ

As illustrated above and across this book, many of the images, similes, and metaphors contained in the poetry of al-Ḥārdallo and other Bedouin poets were eventually assimilated into the poetry of subsequent generations, particularly lyrical poems that were made into songs starting from the early decades of the twentieth century. As such, Bedouin poetry contributed significantly to building the aesthetic and cultural characteristics of the Sudan since those formative years.

3 The Nature Lover

Glorification of nature is evident in a good part of al-Ḥārdallo's verse. His celebration of the advent of the rainy season is replete with nostalgia.

> Confirmed news from home: The Buṭāna plains were hit by heavy rain.
> Pouring all night long, it continued unabated into the morning.
> Male crickets raged with lust; udders, even of young cattle, grew full,
> and she-camels enjoyed a lush meal within a short stroll.

> الخَبَر اَللكيد قالوا الْبُطانة اتّرَشَّتْ
> ساريتنْ تبَقْبِقْ ل الصباح ما انْفَشَّت
> هاج فَحَلْ أمْ صِريصر والممانح بشَّتْ
> وبت ام ساق على حَدَب الْفريق اتعشَّتْ

> Great news from Aḥmad;
> the valley is full to the brim, he said.
> I can't see why we should here stay,
> with no money to spend,
> or a soulmate to drive boredom away.

> الخَبَر اَللكيد الليلة أحمد جابو
> قال الوادي سال واتْقَرّنَنْ تبّابه
> إن سَعَلونا نِحْنَ قْعادنا شِنْ أسبابه
> لا مصروف ولا زولَنْ بِنِتْسَلابه

Last night flashes of lightning set the sky ablaze.
Rumbling thunder played havoc with my homesick heart.
A flock of grouse was cruising around the "Hau" water ponds.
Lightning threaded the Buṭāna dwellings into a long embrace.

البارِحْ بشُوف بِشْلَع بريق النَوْ
وحِسْ رعّادو بنقر في الضمير كَوْ كَوْ
داك كير القطا دوّر مشارع الهَوْ
وفَرْقان البطانة اتْماسَكَنْ بالضّو

One of the most elaborate depictions of nature's beauty is in al-Ḥārdallo's most famous ode "Musdār al-Ṣayd," an imaginary journey across the Buṭāna wilderness, in the company of his most beloved creature, the oryxes. Composed in the latter part of his life while in exile, it was a nostalgic retrospective revealing an outpouring of longing for his playgrounds back at home. It contains lively scenes of the wilderness, captured by a high-definition photographic memory.

Comprising forty quatrains, each providing an independent scene, this poem is a documentary of the oryxes' yearlong wandering after water and pasture. It is a journey across seasons, flora and fauna, and geographical locations of the Buṭāna plains, but it is also a retrospective journey in the poet's homesick soul. These scenes are skillfully threaded together into a grand love story with nature and innocent beauty.

The poem opens with a captivating scene of preparations for a grand reception for rain, a long-awaited guest.

The sun called off its blaze.
Nights traded their simoom for cold breeze.
Lightning filled the sky, sending chills down.
Wings of a darting falcon snapped a tiny bird,
and out of her hiding came the one with charming cheeks.

With that introductory scene, the poet invites us to his "lost paradise," with a close-up on a herd of oryxes.

Expert at choosing their rest and grazing zones,
near branch streams in public they are seen.
Across lush and dry terrain,
all the way from the upper lands they descend.
Meet no harm may they,
to the all-gracious Lord I pray.

That emotional invocation takes us on a ride with those beautiful creatures in a journey through the wilderness. The poet alternates between a tour guide showing us around, a security guard alerting the oryxes to impending danger, and a lover singing the praise of his sweetheart.

Ab-'Arraaq[1] is in full bloom;
Bashandi flowers lending their fragrance to the air.
At the slightest sound, they [oryxes] shrink in fear,
in high terrain they take shelter.
They should now be around Mount al-Gilaiaa umm Ghurra.

Their sharp ears from afar picked a thunder.
A heavy mass of clouds showering on Mount Cartut.
Expansive depressions there sometimes held some water.
May my gracious Lord treat them to a good sip this time.

From Mount Grain they slid toward the heights;
wouldn't wait for the downpour in Biyya and Balous.
A yellow streak running down to their thighbones;
their white skirts are just fascinating.

The deeper they go, the more fervent the poet's supplications grow.

They are already out,
My Lord, always there to respond to every distress call,
I implore You to protect them all,

those short-haired, from every tiny corner gather them.
Not a single one missing.
Every day we come up with a new verse, singing their praise.

Leaving behind Mount Wad Daoul,
the straight-framed in haste pushed ahead,
through the long series of al-Harba plateaus.
At dawn break they were the first arrivals,
at the pools of Ummat Guroud mountains.
How come creatures of such beauty should end up in snares?

The imminent downpour adds a new dimension to the scenery.

Taking a north route from Ummat Rimaila series,
to the east they heard thunder crack,
and clouds spreading their heavy cloak,
flashes of lightning wailing out a loud shriek.
Their leader joined them at dawn break.

In the following couplets, we are introduced to the herd's male leader, courageous and expert at discovering locations of water and good pasture.

Their male leader went about to explore the area,
leaving them behind to graze the *bagail* and *naal*, their favorite meal.
He spotted an overflowing valley.
At Gamzouz some ghosts flickered from the distance.
Around Mount Kaw he found some water.

There they stayed through noon, untroubled.
But once moisture-laden breeze hit their nostrils,
they rose to their feet,
full of longing for their rich pastures of Hagusirwal.
No verse can capture their grace.

Those cinematic images continue in a rhythm that tunes with the motion on the ground, while the poet's fascination with the oryxes' beauty keeps pouring in almost every quatrain.

Though it was the latter part of the day,
they started to prepare for departure.
I can't fill my eyes of their natural beauty,
their dark eyes, untouched by kohl.
After a brief feed on *haweel*, they now feel energetic and fit.
For the likes of me, such a highbred is surely beyond reach.

From afar they shine like white birds.
Thin-haired, molded into perfect figure,
no out-jetting shoulders.
Admirers and singers are mouthful of praise,
for their impeccable beauty and perfect grace.

A scene of warm-hearted reception for the male leaders:

In broad leaps, their male leader went west,
looking for a soft terrain for them to give birth.
He came back to a thrilling reception,
as they gaily lined up ready to set off.

Leaving them at al-Furoukh to stay the night,
in a depression at Um Maymoun he saw green plants.
Though scattered over the highland, they looked lined up as if threaded together.
On seeing him back, they merrily ran down to him like falling leaves.

The poet employs personification across the poem, presenting the oryxes as expectant ladies ready for the "postpartum period."

The Shamal wind presaged the end of rainy season.
Water now only available in depressions.
Only a few days left to delivery and the lying-in month,
those expectant oryxes, in white and yellow like brand textiles,
were back from reed-covered highlands.

Brisk and robust by nature,
their rest place this time of the year,
is the shade of Wad Ḥārir's acacias.
Soon they will give birth to cute babies, soft and hornless.
For their protection against the evil eye I invoke Quranic verse.

Now is time for documenting the special moment.

At Damukiyaat he left them behind.
It must be pleasantly cold around the branch streams of Alfaar valley.
In a cluster of trees intercepted by *hamaraib* plants they gathered.
They were due to give birth any time now.

In the shade of tall reeds they finally gave birth,
breastfed, and wiped hanging fluids off their newborns.
How many solemn, bearded men composed erotic verse,
longing for them, and recalling good old days.

And a "thanksgiving" service:

Praise for their beauty never stopped,
from passed-aways and living alike.
How many before me have admired their dark eyes,
including renowned poet Wad ab-Shawarib.

Another fervent appeal to the Lord:

My Lord, who laid out the earth, erected seven heavens,
created all creatures, both barefoot and shod—
against all evils protect those dark-eyed,
until they steer clear of Mount Baila, no one missing.

The poet's emotions soar high as he comes to draw the curtains on this moving picture. This deep affection for oryxes is consistent with the image of a man who never took part in the hunt for oryxes, which was a prevalent practice during his time, and who never ate oryx meat.

It's not me who would forget them no matter what.
Rain or drought, I never stop composing verse of praise for them.
In tribute of their beauty, son of Zarih[2] and other folks made legendary verse.
From all vermins I implore Saint Sidi al-Hassan to keep them harmless.

Apart from its aesthetic value, "Musdār al-Ṣayd" is an interactive map of the Buṭāna's natural landscape and the change of seasons. It serves as an exhaustive glossary of botanical terms featuring local names of wild plants and trees.

Like all great poems, "Musdār al-Ṣayd" gave rise to different interpretations. Many read it as a "hunting narrative" describing an actual journey for hunting oryxes. This interpretation contradicts with strong historical evidence that al-Ḥārdallo was actually a wildlife campaigner who never engaged in game hunting. His poetry contains numerous references that show how deeply he cared for the oryxes.

Ibrāhīm al-Ḥārdallo was one of those who dismissed the interpretation of "Musdār al-Ṣayd" as a game hunting poem. However, his own reading of it was that the oryxes were used allegorically as a symbol of women's beauty. While the poem does contain allegory in some parts, the musdār as a whole, in my opinion, is a journey in pursuit of beauty as it exists in nature. The frequent evocation of analogies with women is the poet's attempt, consciously or otherwise, to complete a grand portrait of nature in action.

The full text of "Musdār al-Ṣayd" and its English translation appears in chapter 12.

4 Al-Ḥārdallo's Style

The prevalent form of al-Ḥārdallo's poetry is the muraba' or marbūʿ (quatrain), consisting of four lines. His poem is composed of either a single marbūʿ or a combination of those units; the marbūʿ constitutes the vast majority of his verse and addresses broadly diverse topics, while the so-called musdār, a long poem, describes the poet's journey to his beloved. In the case of "Musdār al-Ṣayd," al-Ḥārdallo's most famous work, composed of forty marbūʿ, or 160 lines, it follows the oryxes in their journey across the Buṭāna plains.

The main triggers of al-Ḥārdallo's poetry were perhaps his obsession with beauty, his strong attachment to nature, and the sharp turns in his life. Each one of those factors had a distinctive influence on the content, style, and tone of his verse.

An interesting feature of al-Ḥārdallo's poetry is that his praise of women's beauty is almost always linked to his celebration of the beauty of nature. Throughout his love poems, women are consciously portrayed as a salient feature of nature. The examples are too numerous to enumerate. His praise of a woman's beauty reaches its peak only when it is paralleled to one of the elements of nature, particularly the oryxes and the ductile green cane reeds.

Last night rumors almost split us apart.
But proven false, the fun did start.
Dancing like a cane on the stream mouth,
the stripes on her cheeks have owned my heart.

البارِحْ حَديسْ الناس بِدُور افْرِقْنا
كُلُّو مرَقْ كِضِبْ عُقْبان صِفينا وْرُقْنا

الدرعة أم شلوخاً سِتةّ مالكة عشُقْنا
تتمايخْ مِتِلْ قَصَبة مَناصح الحُقْنه

The same thing happens when the oryx is the focus of his praise. Here also, human beauty is brought to complete the picture.

Leaving them in wait at Ḥajar al-Ṣifayyah,
at al-Dahsaraib he found *gombaar* and cucumber vines.
Are these fascinating oryxes any less in charm,
than necks with gold pendants studded?

خلاّهن على حَجر الصِفَيّة حْبوس
ولقى في الدهسريب قُمبار وعِرْق فَقّوس
في المَخلوقة شِن تشْبه مَعيز امْ روسْ
غير ال في وَريدِن شولَقِن مرْصوصْ

The following piece provides an example of how al-Ḥārdallo's imagery can sometimes be elusive, open to different interpretations.

الليلة المعيز ما ظني أنا ملاقيهن
ناطحات البطين أدَّنْ قِليلَه قِفِيهنْ
سِمْعَنْ طنَّتَ الشادي وكِتِرْ صّنَفيهن
وعند الاصفرار جَفَلَنْ بشوف لَصَفيهِنْ

The renowned Sudanese novelist Tayeb Salih reads a tragic end in the above picture. A herd of oryxes heading to a place of thick trees. Alerted by restless fidgeting of birds, which sense an impending danger, the herd is paralyzed with panic. Before sunset, the expected attack takes place, turning the place into a battle scene, with the oryxes caught up, their yellow colors, mixed with the rising dust, glittering in the horizon.

In the words of Salih, a great admirer of al-Ḥārdallo, "This imagery is as captivating as a painting by an Italian Renaissance artist. A peaceful parade into the bush, then an alarm signal and panic, and then the tragedy engulfs the whole scene, and a whole world falls apart!"[1]

Based on Salih's interpretation, a translation of the above lines can go as follows:

I'll probably not see those oryxes again,
heading toward al-Bitain,
to Gilaila giving their backs.
At the warning sound of restless birds, they wince in panic.
By sunset, they collapse with the sinking sun,
their yellow skins glittering on the horizon.

The other interpretation draws a completely different picture of a broken-hearted narrator agonized by the departure of the herd, which goes into the bush to the twittering of birds, before it sinks into oblivion with the sinking sun.

I'll probably not see those oryxes again,
heading toward al-Bitain,
to Gilaila giving their backs.
Taken away by the twittering of birds, they stop there motionless.
Their amazing color dissolved in the sun's yellow rays spilled on the horizon.

Al-Ḥārdallo's celebration of nature brings to mind some of the most famous Romantic poets, such as William Wordsworth and John Keats. Estranged by rapid change and industrialization, Wordsworth (1770–1850) sought refuge in nature.

My heart leaps up when I behold
A rainbow in the sky:
So was it when my life began;
So is it now I am a man;
So be it when I shall grow old,
Or let me die!
The Child is father of the Man;
And I could wish my days to be
Bound each to each by natural piety.[2]

That same wish was echoed by al-Ḥārdallo in those lines.

Mount Wad Diyab is still inhabited with oryxes.
Their young jubilantly playing around.
Should I with the means be endowed,
I would forsake my own home and choose theirs as my abode.

قوزْ ود ضياب يا اللّيل تَرَى بي شْياهو
بَهَماً بِطَرِّدْ فرحان وعاجبو خلاهو
زولاً في ام قدود المولى كان أداهو
بِقْعُدْ عِنْدَهِنْ بِتْرُك لَهِنْ ماواهو

Also, al-Ḥārdallo's obsession with beauty calls to memory the English poet John Keats (1795–1821). Like his compatriot Wordsworth, "Keats wrote about nature as a source of beauty and as a refuge from the stresses and strains of life in the city. For Keats the world of nature is the closest we can come to an ideal world, a sort of Eden, and is the only real environment that can approach the ideal forms created by the human imagination."[3]

Keats believed that understanding beauty was a means to becoming more acquainted with truth. In the concluding lines of his most famous work "Ode on a Grecian Urn," he writes:

Beauty is truth, truth beauty—that is all
Ye know on earth, and all ye need to know.[4]

In "Musdār al-Ṣayd," al-Ḥārdallo offers a vivid account of the flora and fauna of the Buṭāna plains, and like Keats, he mentions scores of names of plants and other natural objects.

Far from a passive spectator, al-Ḥārdallo was very much a part of the scene, as a narrator, a lover, a player on stage, a guard of that beauty, and a zealous campaigner against game hunting.

To me, "Musdār al-Ṣayd" is a documentary film where lively images are captured by hidden cameras carefully distributed across the wilderness. All the elements of a powerful documentary are present in this grand poem:

passion, vivid imagery, modulation of rhythm, employment of cinematic techniques—such as wide angle, side, and close-up shots—and the ability to weave carefully selected shots into a compelling narrative.

The poem sets an air of expectation right from the outset as the "camera" moves around and takes wide shots.

The sun called off its blaze.
Nights traded their simoom for cold breeze.
Lightning filled the sky, sending chills down.
Wings of a darting falcon snapped a tiny bird,
and out of her hiding came the one with charming cheeks.

الشمْ خوَّختْ بَرَدَنْ ليالي الحرّه
والبرّاق برق مِن مِنّا جاب القِرّه
شوف عيني الصقير بي جناحو كَفَت الفِرّه
تلقاها ام خدود الليلة مَرَقَتْ برّه

From that general scene, the camera closes up on the subject of the documentary: a herd of oryxes.

Expert at choosing their rest and grazing zones,
near branch streams in public they are seen.
Across lush and dry terrain,
all the way from the upper lands they descend.
Meet no harm may they,
to the all-gracious Lord I pray.

تعَرِف لي مشاهيد الرُّقاد والفَرّه
فلاّخ المصب بيهو بْتَبين تِتْورّا
فوق حَيَا فوق مَحَلْ من الصعيد مِنْجَرّه
شاحد الله الكريم ما تلقى فيه مضره

This is followed by a series of vivid scenes of the journey of those beautiful creatures across the Buṭāna landscape, their reaction to the changing weather, and how they cheer at the sound of thunder and the sight of lightning flickering on the horizon.

Ab-ʿArraaq is in full bloom;
Bashandi flowers lending their fragrance to the air.
At the slightest sound, they [oryxes] shrink in fear,
in high terrain they take shelter.
They should now be around Mount al-Gilaiaa umm Ghurra.

أب عرّاق فتق قَرْنو المِبادر شرّا
الباشَندي عمّتْ مهششيب الدِرّه
من النّقْرة كل حين فوق عِليو منصره
ها الايام محاريها القليعة ام غُرّه

Their sharp ears from afar picked a thunder.
A heavy mass of clouds showering on Mount Cartut.
Expansive depressions there sometimes held some water.
May my gracious Lord treat them to a good sip this time.

قَدَمَت من هِنا وبي ضانْها سِمْعت كرّه
فوقْ كارتوت شخيتيراً تِخَيّن خرّ
قلّاتو الوُهاط بِي لُشْغه قَبْلو مَحَرّه
يا باسطَ النعمْ تسقيها في ها المرّه

While the camera is given a free rein to capture the natural landscape, the "script" takes us on a deep dive into the inner feelings of the narrator as he implores divine protection for the oryxes.

They are already out,
My Lord, always there to respond to every distress call,
I implore You to protect them all,
those short-haired, from every tiny corner gather them.
Not a single one missing.
Every day we come up with a new verse, singing their praise.

مرقن يامجيب لي جُملة السُعّال
شاحدَكْ تجمعِنْ من مَطْبَق الحلاّل
ما ينقُّص حساب الدُّرْج ولَو بي عْجال
ونِحنَ نْجيبْ لَهِنْ في كُلّ يومْ مُنْوالْ

And as he praises their beauty.

A yellow streak running down to their thighbones;
their white skirts are just fascinating.

صُفْراً دِرْعَتِن تِدْلّى لا لْبَهّال
وبُيْضَتْ شاشْ قرابين تريعً البال

Early morning from Mount Baila,
they slid in one line, self-guided,
their massive bottoms adding to their allure.

من بيلا الصباح اسّرْبَقَنْ هُمّال
والدوف فوق حقايبْهن كَتَرْتو جَمال

No verse can capture their grace,
no matter how eloquent the poet is.

مابْيات البَلَد دايرات حَقُّو السِّروال
وصفاً متَّع الغنّاي قَدُرْ ما قال

Though it was the latter part of the day,
they started to prepare for departure.
I can't fill my eyes of their natural beauty,
their dark eyes, untouched by kohl.

في عاقِب نِهار سوّنلهن مُرْحال
وعينيهِن خْلَقْهِنْ زُرْقْ بَلا كحّال

From afar they shine like white birds.
Thin-haired, molded into perfect figure,

no out-jetting shoulders.
Admirers and singers are mouthful of praise,
for their impeccable beauty and perfect grace.

لونِن من بعيد متل البليبلي نْضافْ
حُرْد ومَعَصراتْ من شبّة الاكْتاف
لي النْاس البغنولِنْ يجُرّوا القاف
مالياتْ الخشُم من كامِل الأوصاف

At one point, he voices an outcry against oryx hunting.

How come creatures of such beauty should end up in snares?

خِلَقَنْ كيف برمُّولهن دَميرْ حَبَّال؟

The changing scenes, graphic descriptions, and dialogue lend a dramatic touch to the poem. Scenes of the security-conscious herd leader scouting around for safe routes and places of pasture and water, the cheerful reception accorded to him upon return, and scenes of the oryxes in early pregnancy, when their steps are not heavy yet, until they finally give birth in the shade of tall reeds are intercepted by the lively portrayal of the oryxes and captivating analogies with women and elements of nature.

In contrast with his dobait or dobay pieces, where he is predominantly the main actor, al-Ḥārdallo willingly gives the center stage in "Musdār al-Ṣayd" to the oryx and retreats to a back seat. Like a director who goes on stage only at the end of the play to greet the spectators, al-Ḥārdallo closes his poem with an emotional statement.

It's not me who would forget them no matter what.
Rain or drought, I never stop composing verse of praise for them.
In tribute of their beauty, son of Zarih and other folks made legendary verse.
From all vermin I implore Saint Sidi al-Hassan to keep them harmless.

مِن عَوَج الوكِتْ ما بَتْركِنْ وانساهِنْ
فوق حَيَا فوق مَحَلْ دايماً بَجُرُّو غْناهِن

ناسْ ابن الذّريخْ ضَرَبو المثل بي جَناهِن
ومِن كل السوام سيدي الحَسن يِبْراهن

"Musdār al-Ṣayd" is a grand narrative of love with nature and a celebration of peace and beauty. It stands out as the most celebrated example of this uniquely Sudanese journey poem and a benchmark for other poets.

Al-Ḥārdallo's poetry embodies most of the distinctive features of Bedouin poetry that eventually passed on to new forms of lyric poetry, such as the ḥaqība and modern songs. Gemination is common in his poetry. Look at the geminated /r/ sound in *marraqa*, *barraqa*, *zarraqa*, and *tarraqa* and the geminated /y/ sound in *rayyis*, *kayyis*, *sayyis*, and *kwayyis* in the two examples below.

The white-necked oryx around Ellao al-Ni'am mound often seen
has shackled my mind to the glittering beads on her hair.
Her spear, naturally sharp, needs no further grinding,
from close range penetrated me.

دَرْعاتاُ على عليوّ النَعام مرّاقه
دَرَجَتْ عقلي في نجيم عُقْلَته أم **برّاقه**
تَفْ أم إيد نَفِجْ حَرْبَتَه مي **زرّاقه**
حادة برا نَفِخْ فوراً كتير **وطرّاقه**

I yearned for the time when I was my own master,
Riding long distances to reach them [my girlfriends]
to their lips I was expert at finding my way.
That was a time when life was particularly nice to me.

كم شويَمْ لِهنْ وكتاً بفاقِقْ **ورَيّس**
كمْ ودّيت لِهن من عِندي واحدْ **كَيّس**
بسْرِقْ دغْمَتِنْ نَعَمِنّي فيهِن **سَيِّسْ**
دا وكتْ الزمان بِلْحيل مَعانا **كويّسْ**

Al-Ḥārdallo draws his parallels and similes from a rich repertoire taken from the local environment. His meticulous use of these descriptive words demonstrates deep knowledge of the environment. He may use *mi'za* (معزة), *sakhla* (سخلة), or *bahama* (بهمة) in reference to a young oryx, depending on how young it is, while *daifa* (ديفة) refers to more mature oryx, well-developed, in the prime of youth. *Rayhouba* (رايهوبة) is young and attractive; *lakhlukha* (لخلوخة) is a bit fleshy, with heavy steps; while *dar'aa* (درعة) is an oryx with a white or yellow streak running down from her neck. Likewise, analogies with plants vary according to the stage of growth, from *fussaib* (فوسيب), in reference to a thin green cane, to *luttaib* (لُتّيب), which describes a sorghum cane just before bearing fruits.

Al-Ḥārdallo's poetry was a reflection of his time and also his mood. He is the undisputed pioneer of Sudanese Bedouin poetry who established the ethos of this art. The fact that his poetry is still fresh and relevant and widely quoted more than a century after his departure speaks for his legacy.

5 The Musdār

A HISTORICAL CONTEXT

Bedouin poetry as a genre is believed to have entered the Sudan with the migration of Arabian Bedouin tribes to the country, which started as early as pre-Islam and continued into the fifteenth century. In successive waves of migration from the Arabian Peninsula in search of water and pastures, they brought with them a deep-rooted tradition of oral poetry, which played an indispensable role in their daily life. In those largely illiterate communities, poetry was recited and chanted but none of it was preserved in writing. Given the limitations of oral communication, much of that heritage was lost.

There is little evidence to show that the musdār was known before Turkish rule (1820–85). Since the musdār poems, as indeed other forms of folk poetry, were orally communicated, it may be the case that musdārs composed earlier have gone missing. However, researcher Sayed Hamid Ḥureiz is more inclined to see the musdār as a late phenomenon, a more advanced stage in the evolution of Sudanese Bedouin poetry. In his well-documented research work *Fan al-Musdār* (The musdār as an art form), Ḥureiz maintains that narrative poetry, under which the musdār falls, is generally associated with an advanced stage in the development of poetry. "Apparently, that advanced stage which saw the birth of Musdār was during the Turkish rule, as the first versions of Musdārs that reached us belonged to that era."[1]

The three pioneers of this art form were Ibrāhīm al-Farrāsh (1847–83), 'Abdallah Abu-Sin (?–1909), and his brother al-Ḥārdallo (1830–1916). While the brothers were contemporaries of al-Farrāsh, it seems they composed their musdār poems at a later stage of their lives; al-Farrāsh is believed to have died during the Turkish rule, before the Mahdist era (1885–98). Of all the three, al-Ḥārdallo emerged to fame as the undisputed doyen of this art form.

A second generation of musdār poets include Aḥmad ʿAwad al-Karīm Abu-Sin, ʿAbdallah Ḥamad Wad Shawrāni, al-Ṣādiq Ḥamad al-Ḥallāl (wad Āmna), al-ʿĀgib wad Mūsa, and many others.[2] Those poets stayed faithful to the form, content, and technique of the classical musdār. Although some of them eventually quit the nomadic lifestyle and led a sedentary life, their poems continued to reflect the Bedouin spirit and tone of voice. However, references to their new life and to their time found their way to their musdārs. For example, urban words such as *train*, *theater* (*tiyatro*), and *gin* appeared in some of the poetry of Aḥmad ʿAwad al-Karīm Abu-Sin, who settled in Khashm al-Girba and became a farmer.

The word *musdār* in Arabic, مسدار, is the noun for *sadar* (سَدَر), which means to set off on a course toward a certain destination. As a noun, *musdār* means a "known zone" or "destination that cattle go to in search of pasture and water." Each nomadic tribe has certain musdārs, or grazing zones, where they stay for days and then leave to allow other tribes to have their turn. Musdār in this sense is used abundantly in the poetry of the Shukriyah tribe. In his "Musdār Setit," poet ʿAbdallah Abu-Sin has this to say about his beloved, whom he likens to a young oryx.

The young oryx whose Musdār is Jabra,
was talking to me, her words punctuated with sobs.
Nothing will cure me, if I went insane,
except the grapes of the valley of Shobra.[3]

عناق الأريَل المُسْدارها جَبْرَه
تَحَدَّثْني حديثاً كُلّو عَبْرَه
أنا انْ جَنّيت قطْ ما ظَنّي ببرى
بلا عُنّاب جناين وادي شُبْرَه

As a poetry form, musdār refers to a long poem composed of quatrains describing a poet's journey to his beloved. It can be an actual journey, such as the "Musdār of Gouz Rajab" by al-Ṣādiq Ḥamad al-Ḥallāl, or imaginary as in numerous examples. In all cases, it is a love poem describing the poet's yearning for his beloved.[4] The outpouring emotions of longing are punctuated by descriptions of the places met along the road, including the topography and physical features. Such musdārs are named after the starting point of the journey—such as "Musdār Rufā'a," "Musdār Setit," and "Musdār al-Ṣobagh," which describe journeys embarked upon from those places.

Some musdārs describe a yearlong journey to the sweetheart. Rather than highlighting place-names, such poems are more focused on the celestial landscape. They portray images of the changing weather conditions by tracing the movement of stars, and each change in weather signals a step closer to his sweetheart, which enkindles longing. An example of this type is seen in "Musdār al-Nijūm" (The musdār of the stars) by the famous poet Wad Shawrāni. In the following quatrain, he refers to the so-called *al-Naṭiḥ* star, which is associated with the advent of summer.[5]

Al-Naṭiḥ star went down,
leaving us in a stifling heat,
with nights getting shorter and days longer.
I'm longing for the one whose glance emboldened me to defy all laws,
and released streams of songs long blocked inside.[6]

غَابْ نَجْم النَّطِحْ والحَرْ علينا اشْتَدّ
ضَيَّقْنَا وقِصِرْ ليلُه ونِهَارُه امْتَــــدّ
نَظِرة المِنو لِي القَانُون بِقِيت اتّحدي
فَتَحَتْ عِندِي مَنطِقْة الغُنَا الْ انسَدّ

Similarly, in the musdārs that describe places along the journey, the poet sounds desperate to reach the abodes of his sweetheart. The poem is rich in vibrant images of the route the poet takes in the company of his camel, which is no less excited to reach the destination! In "Musdār Rufā'a," Aḥmad 'Awad al-Karīm Abu-Sin explains why his camel was virtually flying to the destination!

In leaps and bounds you flew past Mount Mubārak,
hardly needed any nudge on your belly, a whip, or even a chirrup.
For you surely remember her bounteous generosity,
and how last time you spent the whole time chewing.

ضهير قلعة مبارك جيتو تلعب شدْ
منعْتَ اللسّه والكرباج وقولة هدْ
علَى التالاك إحسان رزقو ما بِنْعدْ
يومك كلو تمْصَعْ ما انلحق لك حَدْ

Hence, it's not only the poet who is burning with longing; the beast, too, has a stake in reaching the destination quickly. And the poet keeps reminding him of the special treatment that will be accorded to him upon arrival.

At one point, 'Abdallah Abu-Sin had to issue a warning to his camel when he noticed that the latter was not up to speed.

What's wrong with you today?
Heavy-footed, lumbering along.
Never ever dream of a rest
before we reach her quarters.[7]

خبّك مو وشيك الليله مالَكْ
تَتَقَّلْ في اليمين وتْجُرْ شِمالكْ
بنَيْتاً لى شيوما بّشْنّي حالَكْ
رُقاداً دونا قطْ لا تْسِيهو بالَكْ

In the following quatrain from "Musdār al-Ṣobagh," Aḥmad 'Awad al-Karīm Abu-Sin tells us how, upon arrival, his sweetheart instructs her aides to take care of her guest's camel as well, while setting the place for their long-awaited reunion.

Take him (the camel) to rest.
Look how exhausted and lean he looks after the long journey.
Bring him food in abundance.
And for us, tidy up the place
I can't wait for my soulmate to heal a wound deep in my heart.[8]

أرُبْطو الجانا ضامر لا كبد لا كرشه
سحّار الغروب جيب لى العلوق بي الورشه
نفِّضَنْ المراتب وطَرّحَنْ بي الفُرْشه
داير يبرى جرحاً في القلب مو خرشه

ʿAbdallah Abu-Sin describes the reception ceremonies when neighbors came down to greet him, and how desperate he was to break free and get to his sweetheart in private.

They unsaddled my greyhound[9]
I had to meet endless waves of greeters and well-wishers.
Deep inside, I was burning with longing,
impatiently craning my neck every now and then
like a hungry camel waiting for his meal.[10]

مشيت وجيت لقيت دلُّو السلوقي
يجوني الناس يِعَجُّو يقيفو فوقي
شاكي الغَلَبه لاكين جدَّ شوقي
مِتِلْ جمل العَلوق كُلْ حين أهوقي

The musdār usually closes with a mood of celebration as the poet—and his camel—enjoy the warm hospitality of their host. Examples of such encounters are the closing quatrains of "Musdār Rufāʿa" by Aḥmad ʿAwad al-Karīm Abu-Sin.

Done with her household chores,
she came in, well-groomed,
reclined on the bed.
My camel wished us good time together:
"Have fun," he called out. "Enjoy a tiyatro game."[11]

قضى من اللوازم وانتحف واتجلّى
كوَّعْ فوق مراتبو وْلى الجلوس اتحلّى
قالع العيص معاند شاية السّلْسِلّه
قال لِيْ معاهو بي لِعِبْ التياترو اتسلّى

I felt indebted to my stud-adorned sturdy beast.
All night long, we lost ourselves in pure rapture.
Her hair was dangling down to her waist.
Only well after the imam had finished dawn prayers
did we surrender to slumber.[12]

أخدْنا الليل تفَنُنْ بي طرب غيرِ عِلّه
تَّمّ كيفي تيس قُنّة اب حديداً شلّه
أنا والديسو لَى عند المتان إدلّى
نومنا بقى لْنا مِنْ بعد الإمام ما صلّى

'Abdallah Abu-Sin's "Musdār Setit" closes with an intimate chit-chat between the poet and his sweetheart once they finally got to each other in private.

In haste I opened the door and dashed in.
There she was—her cheeks glittering like her jewelry.
She's my heart's undisputed choice,
a perfect embodiment of beauty.

فتحتَ الباب دخلْ عجلان عليها
لقيت ام خدْ تنوِّرْ زي حِليها
بِنَيْتاً من زمان شويَمْنا ليها
بشوف خِلَق الجمال مجموعة فيها

Your absence this time was too long, she said.
Three full months, I have been counting.
But since you are here now
stop arguing, let me call you to account.

تقول لي يا ولوف طوّلْ غيابكْ
تلاتهْ شهور تمام معروف حسابك
دحين وكتين حضرْ والمولى جابكْ
أقيف لا تلجلجْ النوريك حسابكْ

What is the point in blaming me, I said
when your passion has taken the best of me.
Stop censuring me and come closer to my heart.
Who else have I been singing her praise?

أقول ليها العتاب لَيْ ليه تَشَنٍّي
زماناً ماهو دا غيٍّك مكنٍّي
اتركي ها العتاب لى روحي دنٍّي
براك لي مَنْ بنوح دايماً واغني

It is striking to note that the camel features prominently in both musdārs, not merely as a means of transport but also as a companion on the journey and even a bona fide friend. Dialogue with the camel is a common feature in Bedouin poetry, as poets find solace in the company of their beasts and confide their emotions to them. Al-Ḥārdallo makes many references to his camels, particularly 'Itayyid and al-Bāngair. However, there is no mention of them in "Musdār al-Ṣayd." It could be because in this long poem, al-Ḥārdallo opted to give the center stage to the oryxes in their fascinating journey across the Buṭāna, with minimum intervention from his side.

The above-mentioned two types of musdārs, which describe the journey on the ground and the journey through the seasons, are discussed in more detail in the following two chapters.

6 Musdār al-Nijūm

A JOURNEY ACROSS THE STARS

Some musdārs describe the poet's yearlong journey across the Buṭāna toward his sweetheart. These musdārs reflect a deep knowledge of the local climate and astronomy and demonstrate the Bedouins' sharp weather forecasting skills.

The Bedouins have their own ways of monitoring weather conditions and the change of seasons. Each of the four seasons is divided into seven *'inas* (represented by stars with designated names). Each star, or *'ina*, lasts for approximately thirteen days and is associated with a certain part of the season. While they presage a change in seasons, the rise and demise of these stars also trigger the poet's passion and longing for his sweetheart.

The journey begins in early summer, with the rise of *al-Naṭiḥ* star, around April 21 each year. The seven *'inas* of summer are *al-Naṭiḥ*, *al-Biṭain*, *al-Tirayya*, *al-Dabarān*, *al-Hak'ah*, *al-Han'ah*, and *al-Ḍurā'*.

A good example of this is "Musdār al-Nijūm" (Musdār of the stars), by 'Abdallah Ḥamad Wad Shawrāni.[1] The twenty-eight-quatrain poem opens with a confession, evoked by the sinking of *al-Naṭiḥ* star.

Al-Naṭiḥ star went down,
leaving us in a stifling heat,
with nights getting shorter and days longer.
I'm longing for the one whose glance emboldened me to defy all laws,
and released streams of songs long-blocked inside.

غَابْ نَجْم النَّطِحْ والحَرْ علينا اشْتَدَّ
ضَيَّقْنَا وقِصِرْ ليلُه ونِهَارُه امْتَـــــدَّ
نَظِرة المِنو لِي القَانُون بِقِت اتَّحدي
فَتَحَتْ عِندِي مَنطِقْة الغُنَي الْ انْسَدَّ

An interesting feature across this musdār is the poet's ability to draw parallels between the changing weather conditions and his ever-escalating longing for his sweetheart.

In the next quatrain, we are introduced to *al-Biṭain* star, which is associated with some drizzles, although the rainy season is still far ahead. A hot weather that drives snakes and insects out of their holes but also evokes powerful emotions of longing for a sweetheart with charming cheeks who is hard to rein in. Drawing on a metaphor inspired by the Bedouin lifestyle, he compares the prospects of winning anything out of her to producing butter from water! Bedouin women pour milk into a goat-skin pouch, tie it off at the end with a rope, and hang it on a tripod. They then rock it for some time to produce butter. In contrast to this fault-proof exercise, the poet's chances of winning favor with his sweetheart are as good as the prospects of extracting butter from water!

Al-Biṭain star is out.
Lightning is striking across the horizon.
Snakes and insects are coming out, gasping for air.
I'm desperate to see a sweetheart whose cheeks glitter like a mirror.
Winning her favor is as hard as making butter out of water.
I miss her direly, but she barely honors her promises,
lending me sleepless nights.

شَالْ بَرْق البِطين رَقَصَنْ دَبَادْبُه ورشًو
وِينْ النايرة -يا خِلَّايْ- مِرايةْ وَشُـــــــو
عَاشقِي العِندُو حَقْن المُويَة ضَايِق خَشُـــو
سَهْرَان فَاقْدو بِي عِلَّيقُو لَيْ وغَشُـــو

With the arrival of *al-Tirayya*, the third star of summer, it is becoming annoyingly hot, and the poet is imploring his love to end their long parting and come to his rescue.

Al-Tirayya is sending down throttling heat.
I can't wait to catch up with my sweetheart,
her tattoo adding glamour to her lustrous complexion.

She means the world to me
and to my sturdy steed,
who spares no energy to get us there.

لِي زَنْقْ الثَّرَيَا الَحرّو أزَّعَج وُضَيّــق
وينْ النَّادِي وَاصْفر وسيِد وِشَاماَ زَيَّــقْ
ذُوقُو اللَّي أَمل دُنْياَ وْكتَير ما فَيَّــقْ
خَرَّتْ مُقْلَة القلَع الرْسَانَة وْهيَّــقْ

Al-Dabarān has announced its presence with glittering flickers of lightning.
But I am still drowned in my insane longing for her.
She's my inspiration, the master of my verse.
She's exhausted my patience, usurped my heart and mind.
Pray, folks, for our reunion.

رِيدًّها الجاب لَهاَ الدَّبَران بِريقاَ لاَمِعْ
مَاَ فَيَّقني اَفكِر فِي مَعَاشْ وُمَطَامِــعْ
سِتْ قافْيةْ غُناىْ الفُوقَها طَارْبَ السَّامِعْ
قَلَّتْ صَبْرِي شَالَت قَلبِي قُول يا جَامِعْ

Al-Hak'ah star released its breeze.
Its lightning reminded me of a face
more brilliant than the Barrati[2] gold jewelry.
Sleepless all night long, I can't get her out of my mind.
My hair turned gray, yet her arrows are not sparing me.

بَرْق الهَكْعَه رَفَّ وْلاَحْ وُفَلَّك رِياحُو
ذَكَّرْنِي البِفُوق دَهَبْ آلَبراتِي سَمَاحُو
الَخَلاَّنِي اقِيم اللَّيل مِلاَقِي صَبَاحُو
بَعَدْ الشَّيبْ خَفِيف الرُوح جَرَحنِي سْلاَحُو

With the rainy season only two stars (or *'inas*) away, clouds start to build and dust storms become a frequent occurrence. A cold breeze presages rain.

Al-Han'ah is up, with storms and rowdy clouds.
Its cold breeze driving heat away.

But I miss a jewel beyond reach,
only a few merchants can buy.

الهَنْعه امْ هَبَايِبْ قَام سِحَابَها مْهدَّرْ
هَوَاها البَارِد اصبح للسَّخانَة مْقَدَّرْ
وينْ دُرْ جَوهَر الحَضَرِي الصُّعُوبتُو تكَدَّرْ
مَمنُوع ما سِهِلْ لِتجَارْتو كُلّ مُسَدَّرْ

Driving a heavy cloud, *al-Ḍurāʿ* lightning brought me a familiar scent,
from the one who's to my ailments a sure cure.
I'm still singing her praise although my hair turned gray.
Truly her passion is irresistible.

دِعَاشْ بَرْق الضُرَاع الفِي السَّحابَه بْـلاَوِي
جَلبْ لَيْ رآَيحَه مِن اللِي أَذَايْ بِتْـــدَاوِي
كان ما الحُبْ صَعَب مِن الكُبَار وُبَـلاَوِي
ما فِيش دَاعِي بَعَد الشَّيب أكون لها راوي

We are now into the rainy season, with its seven *ʿinas*: *al-Natrah*, *al-Ṭarfah*, *al-Jabhah*, *al-Khayrasān*, *al-Ṣarfah*, *al-ʿIwah*, and *al-Simāk*.

The poet draws a scene of anticipation and excitement, with *al-Natrah* star coming out conspicuously on the horizon. This is the day when oryxes usually come out to watch flashes of lightning that presage the imminent rainfall. Yet his own oryx is nowhere to be seen.

Al-Natrah star is up on the horizon
But where is my oryx to come out and watch the lightning?
A high-breed steed,
only to a noble-minded knight she'd give her rein.
Unbearably painful our parting has grown.

نَجْم النَّترةَ فِي شَفَق الحَمَارَات غَـزَّ
وينْ الشَّارْفَه لِي بَرَّاق سِحَابُو الرَزَّ
جِنيبةَ الفارِس الفُوق المَشَمش هَزَّ
فُرْقَها مُرَّ وَدَّرْ من لِساني اللَّـذَّة

Rainfall intensifies with the rise of *al-Ṭarfah*, a period of ceaseless downpour throughout the entire thirteen nights. Yet all this fails to satiate his thirst!

Al-Ṭarfah is copious as usual.
Yet I remain as thirsty as ever for her.
I've abandoned everything, except singing her praise.
I've left my fate in her hands.
It's up to her to cure me or finish me off.

ظَمْيَانِين- وُوَابْلَ الطَّرْفه فُوقنا يِهَطِلْ
مِن الخَلاّ كُلّ عَمَلنا صَار مُتعطِـــلْ
سِيْد تُوه الصِباَ اللي غُنَاهُ مابِنبطِلْ
رَايُو مَعَاهُ يشفي أَلَمْنا وَالــلا يْكَتِلْ

Al-Jabhah is one day longer than the other *'inas* of the rainy season and, like *al-Ṭarfah*, is characterized by a night-long downpour. What is striking about it, as Wad Shawrāni notes, is the fact that it seems to have unlimited reservoir: for all the intensive nightly downpours, the clouds look pretty heavy and dark in the morning, a darkness that reminds him of the hair of his sweetheart.

After a night of intense rain,
the clouds of *al-Jabhah* still heavy remain,
under the glittering flashes of lightning.
As dark as the lush hair of my sweetheart,
the peerless queen of our time,
as bright as the most precious pearls.

الجَبْهَة ام سَوَارِي سِحَابَها بَيَّيتْ مَالِي
بَرْقو الرَقّ ذكّرنِي الوَضِيبَها مَخَالِي
فَرِيدَة عَصْرها وْمَلْكَةْ دَهَرْنا الحَالِي
لُونَها جَواهِر الدُّرْ المَزبَّـــنْ وُّغَالِي

Al-Khayrasān brings intensive lightning and thunder but little rain, and it seems to the poet that the lightning is strong enough to diffuse the clouds, sending down nothing but extreme cold. However, the specter of his sweetheart indifferently walking around in a "light, revealing" dress, braving the cold, lends him warmth.

Al-Khayrasān lightning is piercing through the clouds.
Sleepless I stay watching the dark clouds sending chills down.
My heart, though, is kept warm by a sweetheart
nonchalantly striding about in a light, revealing gown.

بَرْق الخِيْرصَان الفِي السَّحَابه بْشَلِعْ
اسْهَر نُومِي زِيف رُهْبُو البِيبِدي مْقلَّعْ
السَّبَب المِحَرك نَارْ قُلُوبنا تْوَلَّعْ
سَمْحا ماشِي بِي تُوب الدَّلع مُتْدَلِعْ

Just as the big cloud cannot totally conceal the lightning, he is unable to conceal his passion for his sweetheart.

Al-Ṣarfah lightning adamantly flickering from behind the big cloud
has reignited my passion, laid bare my secret.
This young oryx grazing an ever-green terrain
is the only doctor capable of curing my pain.

بَرْق الّصْرفَه شَالْ تِحْتَ السّحابَة وخَتّ
ذَكّرنِي لِيْ مَرَادتا لَيْ أَبَتْ تَتْغـــــــتّ
ظَبْيَ البِى الجَزُو العَسّنْ سَدُوهِن شَتّ
دِكْتُور عِلَتِي اللي غيرهُ ما بْتَنْفَتـــــــّ

The gentle landing of a moisture-laden breeze, followed by lightning and thunder, triggers memories of the gentle strides of his fancy sweetheart.

Breathing out gentle breeze,
Al-ʿIwah leashed lightning and thunder.
It reminded me of her elegant steps,
and my long-festered wounds opened up.
It's up to her now: to restore my soul,
or deal me a fatal blow once and for all.

هَوَا نَفَس العِوَا البَّراقُو رَعَدُو يْصَيِخْ
ذَكّرنِي البِقْدِل وْفِي مَشِيهُ بِمَيِـــــخْ
يِشُوفَ رايُو الفَتَق جَرْحِي الْ اكان مُقَيِخْ
يِحْلم ولا يِكْتُل مَرَّه وَاحْدَه يَرَيِـــخْ

The advent of *al-Simāk*, the last *'ina* of the rainy season, signals the imminent approach of winter. Again, the fluctuating weather conditions continue to enflame the poet's longing.

Toward the end of *al-Simāk*,
autumn is set for departure, giving way for winter.
My eyes are sore and sleepless,
missing my love and her sweet tongue.
Our parting is a sharp sword putting my life in peril.

في آخْر الّسماك ود عيني زَاد لِجليجو
وَالاَهُ الشّتا وَ عْقَّبْ الخرِيف بي عِريجو
فاقد لَعبة المريود وحالي لهيجو
سيفو الحاد حياتي خَتورة من دهّيجو

The musdār continues in the same manner, traveling with the stars of the remaining two seasons of winter and spring. The rise and demise of each star evokes and enflames the pain of parting in the poet's soul. Apart from vivid similes and metaphors, this poem serves as a star chart documenting the changing seasons and demonstrates a deep knowledge of the stars.

7 Musdār Rufā'a

A TERRESTRIAL JOURNEY ACROSS THE BUṬĀNA

Unlike Wad Shawrāni's "Musdār al-Nijūm," which follows the movement of stars and changing seasons, "Musdār Rufā'a" by Aḥmad wad 'Awad al-Karīm is an example of the "terrestrial" musdār, which describes a journey on the ground, bound to the poet's sweetheart.[1]

This musdār is made up of a series of scenes describing the progress of the journey across the Buṭāna landscape. And although the poet acts as the narrator, his camel, al-Balaib, is featured prominently across the musdār, with vivid descriptions of him on the run and sometimes joining the conversation.

The journey starts from Rufā'a al-Rubba, the main urban center for the Buṭāna. Al-Rubba means "melting pot," a place that accommodates a diverse mixture of people from different ethnic backgrounds.

Gaily, al-Balaib set off from Rufā'a al-Rubba,
bound for the one who's tied up my heart,
ductile like evergreen plants irrigated by ox-driven waterwheels,
whose abode is far deep in the Bedouin desert.

رفاعة الرُبَّة قافاها البَليب طَرْبان
وناطْح الْمِنُّو ميثاق قلبي مو خربان
فوسيب السواقي البي الّلدوب شَرْبان
بعيدة بلادو فوق في بادية العُربان

He invokes the blessings of "the men of al-Tāka," in reference to the famous religious saints of the Mirghaniyah sect, in the eastern city of Kasala, nestled at the foot of Mount al-Tāka.

I implore the men of al-Tāka to make it a hustle-free trip.
In vast strides, you darted deep into the desert.
Eager to reach one whose neck is elegantly studded with a golden necklace,
your speed caused the saddle to screech and scream.

رجال التاكا بي جاهن قواسيك هانتْ
مَسَكْ فجّاً عميق والبيدا ليك إدانتْ
علي الفي جيدا متبور البراقي مَبَانَتْ
المَخَلوفة ضجّتْ من دويكَ وْعانَتْ

Like a torrent, he poured
across the plantations and al-Sarraf village.
Like a wolf howling on hilltops;
a high-breed indeed, not a baggage-carrier.

بَلْدات الكموقة وحِلّة السرّاف
جاهِنْ داوي دنيات المسافات راف
يالضيب العلي راس القَلَعْ هرّاف
لاهطَكْ حَرْ شيوم لوْ قْراد ولاهو قْراف

Coming past the Sayyāl and Badīnah,
his plan is to convey us on the next day.
Yes, al-Gomri;[2] get me before noon
to the one to whom your master is heavily indebted.

عقب سيالو قد فوق الحليله بدينا
قصدو الليلة في باكريتو يعدينا
علي بلد العلي سيدك مردّم دينا
أرح يا قمري في باقي النهار ودينا

Swimming at high speed, resisting the rein,
you passed the water reservoirs by the acacia trees.
Your final destination is a chandelier, brilliant and lofty,
as elegant as an oryx leaning on green grass,
Don't you worry, my high-breed; she'll take good care of you.

حفيرات السنط جيتن تعوم بي التنية
ناطح الشمعدانة عديلة مي منحنية
درعات العفا الكبد العسين منتنية
مي لافخاك يا تيس قنة بيك معتنية

After passing Wad Mūsa, Ommat Ragareeg flickered in the distance.
Like a fox that heard a threatening sound, you raced away, your neck fixed ahead.
Your legs flying, your bold piercing into untrodden routes scared me.
You can't afford to disregard the orders of the supreme authority.

عَقَبْ ود موسى شرْف أُمات رقاريق شُفْتَ
بعشوماً سِمِعْ نَقْرْه وقطعْتَ اللفتة
بعد دحَّن جرايدك ومن شقيقك خفت
واغْل الأَصْدَرَتْ أمْر القَضَا والإفتا

Through the valley of ab-Tiboub you swiftly pierced.
Even the dump land around Um Oud reservoir failed to slow you down.
My faithful sweetheart must be expecting us.
Let's speed up. I see sweat pouring down your neck.

إيدين أب تبوب شقيت وعرهن خاتر
جيت لي أم عود تجمع في النقع ماك فاتر
الحافظ حضورك ولي غيابك ساتر
أسرع واغلو يا الجمام قفاك متماتر

The barren land is up upon us and beyond it the *hamaraib* bush.
Swim gently, lest you cut your nose peg.
For a high-bred *annafi*[3] like you, not a *kaharaib*,[4]
reaching the abode of my compassionate soulmate is not a big deal.

ديك الشاقة بانت ومنها الحمريب
عوم براحة أوعى تقطع الدمريب
ود جمل الندم عنافي مو كهريب
ماهو بعيد عليك بلد أم حنانة قريب

He leaped onto the top of Dabbat al-Aasaad.
I implore Saint Hasan to protect my steed from evil eyes,
and get us safely to the soft, mild-mannered,
cute and witty, shining over all her peers.

خرت القدة شب فوق دبة الأساد
حسن شيخ طُرْقي ينْجي التيس من الحُسَّاد
محمود الطبايع لين الأجساد
جميلا بي الظرف فوق النداید ساد

By the forenoon we stopped to rest in a shade.
I took a nap and in my dream saw her,
shy as ever, never divulging a secret.
Tall, with dark kohl-rimmed eyes.

سيت لو مقيلو بي الباكرية في الضقال
خد لي هجسة قم فاقد السحى الما قال
اليبس سراة السرعو ماهو تقال
لطيف قامه أدعج واكحل الأمقال

He flew past the farmland, eschewing a crowd of people around sorghum cellars.
Emerging from a narrow strait, he unleashed his strong legs across the route.
Reaching the one with earrings drowned in the darkness of her hair,
shouldn't take long for al-Gomri, my speeding, teeth-clattering steed.

عقَب الوادي فَزْ من المطيمر وناسو
قطع الشلْخه والدرْبْ بالجرايد داسو
هجّام ابْ وَضيباً عامِتِنْ خُرّاسو
ما هو بعيد على القُمْري الهرج ضَرَّاسو

Some shrubs emerged on the horizon, but the beast passed them so quickly as if his feet were a sewing machine that threaded them together!

The shrubs that rose between spiky *kitir* trees
were soon strung together with the sewing machine on his feet.

Never fear the whip, I told him,
as long as your wheels are rolling fast
to the soft, short-haired oryx.

عقيداتْاً بِبينَنْ مِن كِتيرْ النُّصْ
جاهِنْ كَفُّو زَيْ مَكَنْ الخياطه يرُصْ
على المرناع بريريب الأرايل الحُصْ
عَجَلَكْ تِرّوْ عينك في الشقيق لا تْبُصْ

I don't deserve any lashes, he said.
Can't you see my daring shortcuts?
Knowing that our long-awaited reunion with her is nearing
inspirited me to take a bold dive through al-Dhalma bushy valley.

قال لَيْ الشقيق ما بلقى فيَّ ضريبه
ماك شايفني كُلْ مرّات بجيب لِيْ غريبه
الخلاني ايدْ الضالمه أقوم جاري با
شايف هجمة أم خدّاد بِقَتْ لي قريبه

The feeling that the journey is approaching the end point lent a soft tone to their conversation.

Um Wad'a is already behind us,
You may slow down now, O al-Gomri.
We'll soon catch up with the slender, supple-necked,
who endowed my eyes with sleeplessness.
A narrow strait running between
her imposing bosom and ample thighs.

بعد يا القمري ما وخّرْتَ ايد ام ودعه
برّدْ قِرِبْتَ السمحه ام رقبةً فدْعه
الخلّت عيني اللاجه خاتيه الخدعه
بين ثديينا وارْدافينا رُقاً بِدْعه

Now with her abode coming into sight, the poet shares vivid scenes of a warm reception for him and his companion.

By the prickly stockyard fence at the far end,
park silently and quietly.
My longing for her has torn down my heart and liver.
There she is, seated in the lobby of her "Grand Hotel."

كِتيرات الزريبه الخاتماتْ النادي
ابركْ عندَهِنْ لا تقول سلام يا عادي
السلحاتو قاطعه القلب وفارمه اكبادي
داك إياهو في "قرندُ هُتيل" الغادي

After looking after my beast,
the master of my heart came in, led by a long plait.
She offered me an affectionate welcome.
Two tiny scars glittering in her cheeks
and a necklace dangling on her chest.
Together, dear al-Gomri, we'll relive our youth tonight.

بعد ما أنصف الفي يومو دانى بلودو
دخل طيّبْني سيد ريدي الوضويبو بقودو
الطبق الرشيم ردف السدير بى عقودو
معاهو الليله يا القمري الشباب بنعودو

Done with her household chores,
she came in, well-groomed,
reclined on the bed.
My camel wished us good time together:
"Have fun. Enjoy a tiyatro game."[5]

قضى من اللوازم وانتحف واتجلّى
كوَّعْ فوق مراتبو ولى الجلوس اتحلّى
قالع العيص معاند شاية السّلْسِلّه
قال لِيْ معاهو بي لِعِبْ التياترو اتسلّى

I felt indebted to my stud-adorned sturdy beast.
All night long, we lost ourselves in pure rapture.

Her hair was dangling down to her waist.
Only well after the imam had finished his dawn prayers,
did we surrender to slumber.

أخذْنا الليل تفَنُنْ بي طرب غير عِلّه
تَمَّم كيفي تيس قُنّة اب حديداً شلّه
أنا والديسو لَى عند المتان إدلّى
نومنا بقى لْنا مِنْ بعد الإمام ما صلّى

By forenoon, visitors came to greet us.
They were impressed by al-Gomri's,[6] noble breed and superb traits.
Noting my strong passion for Mihairt al-Khail,[7]
they thanked God who made our reunion possible
after a long parting.

أضحت شمْسنا وجانا البسالِي مْطايب
شاف القُمْري لي سمْح الطبايع جايب
قال لَى مهيرة الخيل أُم عشوقا دايب
قادر جامع الشمل البجيب الغايب

Although Wad Shawrāni's musdār shares the same theme with Abu-Sin's, the former seems more vocal in expressing the poet's emotion, stirred by the movement of stars and changing climatic conditions. It is a retrospective journey, spanning the whole year, while Abu-Sin's is much shorter, lasting for only a few days, and more dynamic, rich in dialogue and imagery. Unlike Wad Shawrāni's poem, where there is no mention of the camel, conversation with the beast occupies a prominent space in Abu-Sin's. Both poets, however, were clearly inspired by al-Ḥārdallo in many respects, particularly in their use of imagery and similes and drama.

8 The Role of Bedouin Poetry in Shaping Sudan's Aesthetic Taste

One of the most widely circulated theories about the arrival of Arabian tribes in the Sudan dates it to the pre-Islamic era. In his anthology of Sudanese poetry in the twentieth century, Muḥammad al-Wāthiq writes: "There are conflicting views on the language of the Buṭāna. The prevalent view is that it is the ancient, pre-Islamic Arabic language that entered the Sudan along with the early waves of migration of the Arabian tribes of Rabī'ah, Juhaynah, and Kināna. Due to the isolation of the Sudan from the Arabian Peninsula, that language lived in isolation and continued to preserve some of the ancient vocabulary that perished elsewhere. However, through interaction with the local environment, it assimilated vocabulary from local languages of the Beja and Nubia."[1]

A different opinion, espoused by the late 'Abdalla al-Ṭayyib, claims that the Buṭāna language is a branch of the mother Semitic language, just like Hebrew, Arabic, and Ge'ez. Al-Ṭayyib's opinion is based on a Torahic tradition that Noah's son, Ham, had in fact landed in Ethiopia (the ancient name of Sudan, according to al-Ṭayyib) and embedded his Semitic language there.

Upon the birth of the Funj Islamic State (1500–1821), known as al-Salṭana al-Zarqa, or the Blue Sultanate, the lingua franca was a colloquial Sudanese language born out of the ancient pre-Islamic Arabic.[2] Although, according to al-Wāthiq, the standard Arabic started to flourish with the arrival of scholars and leaders of Sufi orders from different parts of the Islamic world who were attracted by the emergence of the new Islamic state, the poetry scene continued to be dominated by a hybrid form, a combination of the classical Arabic and the colloquial. The short poems of the famous saint Sheikh Faraḥ wad Taktūk, for example, were highly popular at the time, thanks to the poet's amazing ability to translate social and religious messages into witty and powerful verse, full of humor and satire, that automatically won the hearts of locals and grew to become deeply embedded in the Sudanese culture of the present day.

The demise of the Funj State in 1821 marked a new era in the Sudan's history, with the arrival of the Turco-Egyptian administration, which ruled the country for six decades until it was wiped out by the Mahdists. Putting an end to the Mahdist revolution (1885–98), the Anglo-Egyptian rule (1898–1956) laid the foundations of a modern state in the Sudan: a central government, civil service, taxation system, and civil education. The country opened up to external cultural influence. Egyptian Sharia judges and Arabic language teachers were dispatched to the Sudan, and Sudanese students were sent on scholarships to Cairo. That period also saw Europeans establishing their own communities in the Sudan and introducing a new lifestyle (clubs, music, theater) and even rising to the position of governor general.

Al-Wāthiq notes that although standard Arabic became the formal language of the new state during that period, "the dobait reached new heights thanks to genius poets from the Ja'aliyīn, Shukriya, Jamū'iya, and Batāhīn tribes. The Buṭāna region in eastern Sudan became the hub of this art genre and played a central role in shaping the aesthetic taste for the Sudanese people, in harmony with the religious temperament created by the Funj's populist Sufism."[3]

Al-Wāthiq believes that dobait reflected the pulse of the nation more accurately than classical Arabic poetry. To him, dobait served as a record of social life and political developments in the Sudan. It covered such important events as the invasion of Muḥammad Ali Pasha's army; the murder of his son Ismail in the hands of the Ja'aliyīn leader al-Mak Nimir, and the latter's escape to Ethiopia; the heavy-handed Turkish rule; the Mahdist rule and defeat of the Turks; the British invasion; and many more. In contrast, many of classical poets who had served as mouthpieces for the Mahdist rule weirdly kept silent about many important events, such as the defeat of the Mahdist forces in 1898 by Lord Kitchener and the subsequent killing of Calipha 'Abdullahi and the leader Wad Habbuba. A few decades later, major events such as the 1924 upheaval against the British and the trial of national hero Ali 'Abd al-Latīf went virtually unmentioned in classical poetry.

On the impact of the different political and literary ideologies in the poetry of post-independence Sudan—such as socialism, Marxism, Islam, realism, surrealism, existentialism, and structuralism—al-Wāthiq describes them as "superficial masks camouflaging a genuinely Sudanese identity rooted on the populist Sufism of the Funj era and the aesthetic taste of the Buṭāna." Although he admitted that certain poets could be branded as products of a Bedouin environment (such as Muḥammad Sa'id al-'Abbasi, 'Umar al-Banna, 'Abdalla al-Ṭayyib, and Muḥammad al-Mahdi al-Majzoub), while others (such as al-Tijāni Yūsuf Bashīr, Muḥammad Aḥmad Maḥjūb, Aḥmad Muḥammad Ṣaliḥ, and Ṣalāḥ Aḥmad Ibrāhīm) are identifiable with the urban environment, "all of them, in the final analysis, could be traced back to a common root: the Funj and the Buṭāna."[4]

Fascination with the Bedouin environment is particularly evident in the poetry of al-'Abbasi, one of the great twentieth-century poets in the Sudan and the Arab world at large. He was born to a prominent Sufi family. His grandfather Sheikh Aḥmad al-Ṭayyib was the founder of the Sammaniyah Sufi Order in the Sudan. After attending the Khalwa Quranic school, his family sent him to Egypt where he attended a military school, but he deserted it two years later. Back in the Sudan, he spent a good part of his life roaming the plains of Kordofan and Darfur on camelback, intermingling with the Bedouins and singing the praise of the innocent beauty.

May heavy-laden clouds greet you, O Mellit,
with abundant shower on your orchard-rich valley.
Your charming sceneries drive boredom away,
the best cure for a raging thirst.
Upon reaching you we forget,
all pain of travel on backs of speeding beasts.
Your sand dunes: what a striking scene!
Relief for the heavy hearted, and sustenance to those in need.
Your lofty palm trees have no trouble kissing the cloud's tail—
and with the rising dunes around them—
they appear like army flags on mountaintops.
Running water streams are shining like unsheathed swords,

pigeons cocooning on rich shades,
and the breeze driving dancing branches to each other's embrace.
If I were to bestow eternity on one thing on this earth,
it would surely be this place.

حيّاكِ "ملّيطُ" صوبُ العارضِ الغادي
وجاد واديكِ ذا الجنّاتِ من وادِ
فكم جلوتِ لنا من منظرٍ عَجَبٍ
يُشجي الخليَّ ويروي غُلّةَ الصادي
أنسَيْتِني بَرْحَ آلامي وما أخذتْ
منا المطايا بإيجافٍ وإيخاد
كثبانُكِ العفرُ ما أبهى مناظرَها
أُنسٌ لذي وحشةٍ، رِزقٌ لمرتاد
فباسقُ النخلِ ملءُ الطرفِ يلثم من
ذيلِ السحابِ بلا كدٍّ وإجهاد
كأنه ورمالاً حوله ارتفعتْ
أعلامُ جيشٍ بناها فوق أطواد
وأعينُ الماءِ تجري من جداولها
صوارماً عرضوها غيرَ أغماد
والوُرْقُ تهتف والأظلالُ وارفةٌ
والريحُ تدفع ميّاداً لميّاد
لو استطعتُ لأهديتُ الخلودَ لها
لو كان شيءٌ على الدنيا لإخلاد

Al-ʿAbbasi, to al-Wāthiq, is a classic example of a twentieth-century poet composing in standard Arabic yet deeply inspired by the Bedouin environment. He was so obsessed with that environment that some of his standard Arabic poems were tuned to the *jarrāri*, a song structure that echoes the rhythm of camel movement and is popular in Kordofan and Darfur, where the poet had spent many years.

Despite large-scale urbanization, the majority of the Sudanese population is still emotionally attached to their rural, essentially Bedouin, roots. This may explain why the ḥaqība and other folkloric songs have continued to be celebrated for almost a century now. Part of the allure of these songs emanates from the fact that they share with Bedouin poetry not only the settings but also the underlying themes, such as praise of beauty and nostalgia.

The influence of the Bedouin aesthetics can be felt even in modern songs set to orchestral music. Muḥammad al-Amīn, one of Sudan's most renowned musicians, sometimes adds a Bedouin flavor to his music. One of his songs, "Huruf Ismik" (The letters of your name), is a love message in which the poet tells what his soulmate's name means to him.[5]

In the letters of your name,
I read glad tidings,
feel peace of mind,
and enjoy a deep rest after a tough trip.
In the letters of your name,
I see stars landing on jasmine branches,
a flash of joy in beautiful, grief-tainted eyes,
bracelets in the wrists of a little girl,
reading from her small bible.

حروف اسمك
جمال الفال
وراحة البال
وهجعة زول بعد ترحال
حروف اسمك
نجوم ركت على الياسمين
فرح في عين جمالها حزين
أساور في ايدين طفلة
بتحفظ في كتاب الدين

The next couplet adds to the jovial ambience of the song.

In the letters of your name,
I see two lovers united in marriage
after a long parting,
amid cheers and best wishes from kind hearts.

حروف اسمك
زفاف عاشقين بعد فرقة
وسط باقات دعا الطيبين

To help intensify the celebrative mood for this couplet, al-Amīn weaves into the song a musical phrase that echoes part of a popular song performed by girls during wedding rituals. Addressing the bridegroom during the parade to the bride's house, the girls chant:

May this path bring you glad tidings.
May good fortune lead your way,
and guard you from behind.

الليلة العديل والزين
والليلة العديلة تقدمو وتبراه

In "Zawarq al-Alḥan" (Melodies boat), another song by al-Amīn, a couplet opens with these lines:

The eyes of my love are open courtyards flooding with passion,
a message from the depth of soul; an ecstatic chant
a children's tale, a Negro dance,
two lines of *dobait* chanted in a summer night.

عيون حبيبى ديار ساحاتها حنية
رسالة من الروح . . . أنشودة صوفية
حكاية للأطفال . . . أو رقصة زنجية
بيتين من الدوبيت في ليلة صيفية

When the singer finishes the closing line, the accompanying orchestra music fades away except for a solo violin, which follows the singer as he repeats that line. The melody of that particular line immediately adds a Bedouin air to the song as it evokes images of Bedouins listening to dobait poetry on a moonlit night.

9 The Bedouin Poem

A LIVING LEGACY

During the first half of the twentieth century Bedouin poetry managed to spill over beyond its territory into the sedentary communities and urban centers of the time. A major manifestation of this impact can be seen in the evolution of lyric poetry in Omdurman from the 1920s to the 1950s. Now one of the three towns that make up the Sudanese capital Khartoum, Omdurman was created by Muḥammad Aḥmad al-Mahdi in 1885 following his victory over the Turco-Egyptian administration. He made it the capital of his newly established Islamic state, which remained intact until it was conquered in 1898 by the Anglo-Egyptian forces. Omdurman, however, developed into a melting pot for the different ethnicities that settled during and after the Mahdist era.

As virtually all of the inhabitants of the newly established community had moved in from across the country, the prevalent culture in Omdurman was by necessity a Bedouin one, as manifested in architecture, lifestyle, and artistic expression. The only song form at wedding events was the dobait, a Bedouin lyric genre par excellence. Dobait quatrains were chanted by a lead singer, with a chorus (*ṭanābra*, sing. *ṭanbāri*) behind him uttering throaty sounds yet no musical or even percussion instruments. Like Bedouin poetry, the predominant themes of the dobait lyrics were pain of parting and praise of beauty and virility.

A typical setting for a wedding party is a spacious courtyard, with the men on one side, most of them standing, while the women are seated on *angaraibs* (wooden frame beds) or on floor mats on the opposite side with their backs to the wall, and the singer standing at the front. A long straw mat carpet is laid at the center to serve as the dancing stage. Once the singer starts, the bridegroom or relatives invite girls into the dancing circle and only at this point can the singer and the audience catch a glimpse of the girl in the light of the *ratina*, a big white-kerosene-fueled lamp placed on a long stand.

Starting in the second decade of the twentieth century, the *ṭanābra* that stood behind the lead singer and uttered throaty sounds as part of the song were replaced by others who clapped in rhythm and repeated the opening couplet of each song. That marked the birth of the so-called *ḥaqība*, a unique genre of Sudanese music and lyric poetry that dominated the scene for many decades and is still celebrated across the country. Poets attended most of those events and were seated in the first line of men and a good number of the lyrics of the ḥaqība were born out of those wedding parties.

While the ḥaqība as a song was influenced by the *madīḥ* (Sufi songs in praise of Prophet Muḥammad), the lyric style of both have strong roots in Bedouin poetry. The theme of yearning dominant in Bedouin poetry is central to both the madīḥ and the ḥaqība song. Just as the Bedouin poet is driven by longing for his love to embark on a journey across the desert, so is the madīḥ poet eager to reach the holy shrines of Mecca and visit the mosque and grave of the Prophet in al-Madinah.

Addressing Prophet Muḥammad, Hāj al-Māḥi, a famous madīḥ poet and chanter, opens one of his poems with the following emotional cry:

My longing for you has burnt my heart
I wish I could fly to reach you.
Your love has struck me
from a very young age, O Bashir[1]

شوقك شوى الضمير
أطراك مناي أطير
أنا حابك من صغيــر
بريدك يالبشيــر

Echoing similar sentiments, lyric poet Ṣālih ʻAbd al-Sīd Abu-Ṣalāḥ calls out to his sweetheart.

Come to my rescue,
my young oryx.
I'm lost in your dark eyes.

يا رشا يا كحيل غيثنى
الهـــــــــوى سباني

My heart is sick with longing,
for the heavenly gleam in your cheeks.
Your flames are consuming me,
and your arrows hitting from east and west.
Adding to my torment, your waist,
lean and narrow under an imposing chest,
is swaying like a young ben tree.

يا المرضنى وما طبانى
في خديدك يلوح نور رباني
نيران أشواقك لاهبانى
وسهام ألحاظك ناشبانى
ومن ضمن الحاله التاعبانى
مهضوم كشحك صدرك باني
يتهادى يميل خصرك فريع باني

Since your spell struck me,
sleep deserted my eyes, and passion took hold.
Your troops ransacked my stronghold,
their shelling never missing their target.
Your waist dances in tune with your swaying breast.
Your shoulders reeling under a fruit-laden twig.

من شفت الحسن الفتاني
نومي ترحل ووجدي اتانى
مال جيش حبك عتانى
بى سهامو الما بتختانى
ومال صدرك ولحشاك تانى

كتفك مال به فريع بستاني
يتل في دروعه يغوص تاني

Abu-Ṣalāḥ's lyrics draw heavily from Bedouin poetry, particularly in expressions of longing and in likening his love to oryxes and ductile green plants and her glittering smiles to flashes of lightning.

No other oryx
can usurp my heart and mind.
Who on earth can decode
the charm of a heavenly star like you?

صيدة غيرك ايه الجسّرا
تستلم افكارنا و تأسرا
حال محاسنك مين الفسّرا
يا الثريا الفوق اهل الثرى

Your body struggling under your chest's weight.
Your bosom playing havoc with my heart.
Use your hair strands reaching down to your toes
to collect my heart shards scattered at your feet.

الصدير أعطافك فتّرا
النهيد باع فينا واشترى
الشعر اقدامك ستّرا
لَقِّطِيبُو قلوبنا البَعْثَرا

Likening of his sweetheart to a ben tree is repeatedly seen in Abu-Ṣalāḥ's lyrics.

A young ben branch dancing with the breeze
imitating the swaying beauty on the dancing stage.
My heart readily catches fire from the beauty scars
glittering in her cheeks and gleaming smiles.

فريع البانة المِنْ نسمة
يتمايل حاكى المنقسمة
نار قلبي بتوقد من وسمه
تلمع في خديدا وفر بسمه

Abu-Ṣalāḥ is fond of imploring the breeze to use his "good offices" (meditation) with the beloved, as in the following poem.

Shuttling back and forth,
the breeze is lost,
between the nonchalant heart of hers,
and the longing heart of mine.

من قليبو الجافي لي قليبي الحان
النسيم يتردد عامل استمحان

From her grapevine,
tree twigs are sipping glassfuls of wine.
And from their seats on jubilant, swaying branches,
birds are intoning sweet twitter.
Flowers are joining the choir,
and basils dancing their way to the stage.

الغصون تتناول مِنٌّو خمر الحان
والطيور تتناشد رايقة الالحان
الفروع بتميّل ميلة الفرحان
الزهور بتصفّق ويرقص الريحان

O breeze,
flattering with my ben tree,
causing her stem to dance and sway.
Oh dear,
enjoying her company,
while I am on fire!—
would you identify my ailment

and prescribe a treatment?
A serious wound? A snake bite? What?

يانسـيم مابـالك تثـني قـامة البان
انت رايـق تلـعب والعشوق تعبان
اكتشف ما دائي ومااليدوا الصـعبان
هل دا جرحاً بالغ ام دا سم ثعبان

"You will have to live with it," the breeze said.
"My fragrance can't do you any good,
not even the wisdom of Saint Luqman can.
The only cure to your wounds, sick man,
is the aloe nectar of her pomegranates."

قال لي لازم صـبرك مُـدة الازمـان
لاروايـحـي تطِـبّك لا ولا لـقمان
البداوي جـروحك شـفتو يـا سقمان
في عـصير الند البنـضحو الرُمّان

Apparently losing hope in the ability, or willingness, of the breeze to help him, the poet turns directly to his beloved.

Your passion has occupied me, driven all dwellers away,
filled all corners of my inner soul.
All flames would feel like a pleasant breeze,
if our two hearts were to come together in unison.

بـي غـرامـك حـلّ ورحّل السكان
في مدائن جـوفي تمـلّك الاركـان
ما ألـذّ النـار السـارجة بي لوكان
يبقا قلبي وقـلبك في الغرام شركان

Your eyes are serene and inviting,
but the swordsman at their gate is sober and alert.
Your eyelashes are sharp enough to strike down bold knights.

A luminous moon in a human form,
you took to yourself the beauty of the whole world;
I went away with the miseries of all poets.

صاحي سيّاف لحظك والطريف نعسان
ليك رشـرش قاطع جندل الفرسان
انـت بـدراً سـاطع في قوام انسان
ليـك حسن الدنيا ولي شعر حسّان

In the following poem, he restlessly shuttles between the breeze and his sweetheart.

Aromas wafting from her direction triggered my sensations.
Do me a favor, O night breeze,
go back to her.
Tell her my love for her is shattering my heart.
For God's sake, who created both of us, O breeze,
go deliver this message and let me know her response.

هبتلى روايح داهشانى
يا نسيم عقب عود على شانى
قول ليه غرامك اغشانى
وادركنى الدمع الرشانى
حسنك شانك والحب شانى
يا نسيم روح بلغ واغشانى
بى حق من أنشاك وانشانى

I am your prisoner, my guardian angel.
You are bathing in your gleaming beauty.
I'm burning in my passion fire.
It's my eyes who are to blame
cause they plunged me into your perilous sea
and offered no help.

إيه يا ملاكاً حسنه سجانى
ليك نوره ولى نار سارجانى
طرفي اللمحك هو الجاني
في بحور أشواقك زجانى
فيك خاطر بى وما نجانى

Flames of longing are soaring high,
even my ceaseless tears can't quench them.
I'll never forsake you even if you do.
My eyes lured me into the snares of your beauty
I'm still locked in, all alone,
with no companion except my longing.

جمر الأشواق هب قلاني
ما أنطفا بى دمعي البلانى
أنا لا اسلاك لو تسلانى
طرفي لى محاسنك دلاني
ملكني هواك وخلاني
فارقت أقاربي وخلاني
حسنك والاك والحب والاني

10 The Musdār and the Ḥaqība

Another important theme the ḥaqība seems to have borrowed from Bedouin poetry is the motif of journey, as exemplified in the musdār. Ibrāhīm al-ʿAbbādi, a pioneer ḥaqība poet, describes a journey with friends to the town of Sinja in south central Sudan.[1] Rather than a camel, their means of transport was a Fiat! But apart from that difference, the poem reflected the same air of expectation and excitement prevalent in the Bedouin musdārs. Here we are introduced to a high-spirited Fiat driver and a car flying at such a speed that big trees looked as blurred images. This calls to memory a similar scene by the Bedouin poet Aḥmad ʿAwad al-Karīm Abu-Sin, describing how cheerful and energetic his camel was, leaping across the wilderness.

In leaps and bounds you flew past Mount Mubārak,
hardly needed any nudge on your belly, a whip, or even a chirrup.
For you surely remember her bounteous generosity,
and how last time you spent the whole time chewing.

ضهير قلعة مبارك جيتو تلعب شدْ
مَنَعْتَ اللِسّه والكرباج وقولة هدْ
علَى التالاك إحسان رزقو ما بِنْعدْ
يومك كلو تمْضَعْ ما انلحق لك حَدْ

While Abu-Sin reveals the secret behind his beast's enthusiasm, al-ʿAbbādi opts to leave it to our imagination! The only hint he gives is an appeal to the driver to slow down "by Hunda's quarters." In this poem we meet the same elaborate description of the route and vivid accounts of the events encountered during the journey, including dogs chasing the car and an unusual encounter with a group of young girls who were so open and friendly they offered to help the poet satiate his thirst from their palms!

Slide along the river route,
O Fiat driver.
But remember to slow down by Hunda's quarters.

يا سايق الفيات قوم بي واخد سنده
بالدرب التحت تجاه ربوع هنده

Shooting through the land,
you've outraced our fleeting thoughts.
Lean toward the river, O Fiat,
but make sure not to scare the herds,
or shock the yellow-streaked oryx.

اطوي الأرض واضرع
من أفكارنا سيرك يا الفيات اسرع
ميل على المشرع
لا تريع القطيع بتجفل الادرع

The Fiat driver is high-spirited today.
His speeding beast has reduced huge trees to blurred images.
But where are you heading to?
You went on the wrong route!
Keep right to al-Rammash exit!

شوف سايق الفيات الليلة كيفن هاش
والشدر الكبار بقى شوفنا ليهو طشاش
قول لي دحين وين ماش
فارقت الطريق اتيامن الرماش

He pierced through the mainland,
leaving the households to his right.

The chasing dogs captured nothing but dust.
Sunset must be only a few minutes away,
the Shallal mushra'a[2] has come into view.

شقا حشا الطريق واتيمم الحلال
زفنوا الكلاب ما نالن الا علال
فاضلات ثواني قلال
بين الغروب داك مشرع الشلال

Behold the river,
running solemnly, almost in slumber,
a standing testimony to impeccable divine power,
to which man stands as ungrateful as ever.

شوف النهر مار بي خشوع تقول هجسان
أو مر المنام بي مقلة النعسان
جلت قدرتو ما اكفر الإنسان
كم ينسى الجميل كم يجحد الإحسان

Dismount here, Sarour,[3] and feel the power of creation.
See a natural beauty untouched by powder.
Bewitched by a flock of girls at the shore,
I don't know,
if it was from the tan or the brunette color
I received the fatal blow.

انزل يا سرور وشوف يد القدره
وشوف حسن البداوة الما لمس بدره
وراد النهر أردوني ما بدرا
كاتلني الصفار ام نضرة الخدره

As though we were long acquaintances,
the girls didn't shy away when we approached.
"I am thirsty but can't find a cup," I said—
and the bluff worked well.

“Never mind,” they said.
“Come drink from our palms till you’re full.”

ما نفرن تقول سابق الكلام إلفة
عطشان قلت ليهن وصحَّت البَلْفَه
مافيش كاس قريب قالَنْ بِدون كُلْفه
تشرب بي كِفوفنا لمّا تِتْكفي

The closing couplet echoes the similar cheerful mood of the Bedouin musdārs discussed earlier, when the poet reaches his destination and reunites with his sweetheart.

11 Contemporary Musdārs

The musdār tradition seems to have found a local hold in present-day urban centers. Many contemporary poets have taken the musdār to new levels, addressing new themes in a way that demonstrates high sensitivity to current issues.

An interesting example is "Musdār Abu al-Surra lil Yanki" (Musdār of Abul Surra to the Yankee), by Muḥammad Ṭāha al-Gaddāl.[1] Triggered by the 1982 Sabra and Shatila massacre in Beirut, this poem narrates a parade bound for the Statute of Liberty in New York, in which all of the earth's creatures demonstrate against the United States (the Yankee), for its alleged role in encouraging the Israeli invasion of Lebanon and instigating the massacre.[2]

Although this highly symbolic poem is a clear departure from the traditional themes of Bedouin poetry—namely love, longing, and pain of parting—it does employ the same structure of the Bedouin musdār and the same Bedouin spirit and tone of voice, which becomes particularly clear when the poem is recited. Any local Bedouin who listens to it is likely to miss the subtle symbolic references but will find himself enraptured by the authentic Bedouin ambience created by the dialect, tone, sentence structure, and even body language.

The poet skillfully sets the mood of the poem right from the beginning, and one technique he employs is fusion of consonant sounds, which helps in creating an atmosphere of rage and tension. This is observed in the opening lines where the consonant ن /n/ sound is geminated in the rhyming words at the end of line.

أماتى القبيل بى حِنَّهِنْ **لجَّنِّي**
كَرْفَه وقَلْدَه كيف شوق اللبن **رَجَّنِّي**!!
حزناً جانِي فى ميع الصبا **يلجِنِّي**
أطلع منِّي يا جلْدى المنمِّل **جِنِّي**
وأطلع منى ياحزناً بقى **مكجِنِّي**

[ummāti al-gibail bai-ḥinnahin **lajanni**
karfa-w-galda kaif shōg al-laban **rajanni**
ḥuznan jāni fī maya' al-ṣiba **yalajinni**
aṭla' minni yā jildi l-minammil **jinni**
w-aṭla' minni yā ḥuznan biga **makachinni**]

In the laps of compassionate mothers,
I was cradled and cuddled.
Now in the prime of youth, in the throes of a paralyzing grief I'm strained.
Oh skin of mine;
oh grief that distastes me:
Get out of me.

Consonantal gemination is a technique borrowed from Bedouin poetry and passed on to the ḥaqība and more modern lyric poetry. It enriches the musicality of the verse, particularly when used in the rhyme word as in the above example.

Tension builds up gradually as the compassionate mothers vainly try to dissuade the frustrated poet from leaving his homeland, and the poet encourages his friend to join him.

"What"—my mothers asked—"brought this idea of traveling to your mind?
Use your sense of judgment:
Which is harder:
the nightshift work here,
or humiliation by the Arabian Bedouins?
You hardly lack anything here.
You have a good stock of clothes of all sorts.

Which is better: festive seasons here or humiliating life in exile?
Your dreams are flashes of lightning,
that may presage rain, but may yield nothing."

What is the point, Abul Surra,[3] in staying here,
in the shades of huge buildings fitted with outdoor surveillance cameras?
Life has grown colocynth bitter.
Even our stock of snuff ran out,
leaving us with no option but to use snuff balls over and over again.
It has grown insanely tight, with nowhere left to go.
Should we turn to the land of freedom?

In the following couplet, the poet quotes the opening lines of al-Ḥārdallo's "Musdār al-Ṣayd," which draw a scene of the Buṭāna plains celebrating the arrival of the rainy season, a celebration in which even the sun connived, tempting "the one with charming cheeks" (a reference to the oryx) to come out of her hiding. Here al-Gaddāl uses "the charming cheeks" figuratively as a reference to the beloved homeland or as an abstract value (patriotism). The protagonist comes to her rescue, cleanses "the Yankee" off her eyes, and they chest swim into the sea. From this point, the poet and his sweetheart begin mobilizing for their parade.

(*The sun called off its blaze.*
Nights traded their simoom for cold breeze.
Lightning filled the sky, sending chills down.
Wings of a darting falcon snapped a tiny bird,
and out of her hiding came the one with charming cheeks.)[4]
The one with charming cheeks is out to make a fenugreek pie
to build more flesh on her thighs.
The pasteurized milk is made by the Yankee.
The dry dung fuel hurts our eyes and lungs.
What's the benefit of fenugreek pie,
when the real fuel was taken away by the Yankee?
Out of the blinding smoke she rose,

and polished her face.
The Yankee was lurking for her,
in the blind mirror of the night.

I found her, like a fledgling bird;
her pupils protruding; shivering with fear.
She steered clear of him and fell on my arms,
her chest boiling.
I saw the Yankee in her pupils, Abul Surra.
I took her down to the sea to cleanse the Yankee off her eyes.
Crossing the seawall, we chest swam into the sea.
Swimming underwater for a distance
all the way through the route of love, we saw no stranger.
Everyone was familiar to us.
Frogs, tilapias, and tiny fish led me to the crocodile.
We called out to the mud workers: earthworms, catfish, and tadpoles.
They were asleep in the guard of calf fish,
between two rocks and the shade of a smooth stone.
Together we set off.
The awakened mud workers collected sea gravels and gave everyone seven pieces.
The road-expert mud workers led us to light.
There we found a whole world waiting for us:
cooing turtledoves, shrieking hawks, and howling falcons.
And the mud workers mingled with desert experts:
hill gravels, cobras, lizards, and downtrodden people.

Tension soars against the backdrop of the massacre, and a mobilization of all creatures on earth starts.

Look closely, Abul Surra,
to distinguish the good from the evil,
the true from the false.
Look closely, Abul Surra,
stick your index finger

in the looter's face.
Relax the rein of the highbred steed.
Having traveled throughout the day, Abul Surra,
We're well on course.
The mud workers expertly led us to the harbor of light.
There we found a whole world waiting for us:
cooing turtle doves
shrieking hawks
howling falcons
and the mud workers, the route experts.
A big crowd:
reptiles
livestock
sea farers
birds.
The cloud above our heads,
was keeping an eye on the Yankee's tail.
"Be alert," the turtledove said to the cloud: "Never lose sight of the Yankee."
The snake said: He can't run away from me.
Before sinking in the horizon, the sun said to the sharp-sighted hawks:
Stay on full alert.
We saw in the distance circular straw shacks.
"Skip them," said the lizards.
"Those Arabian Bedouins are tails of the Yankee."
The crowd concurred: Skip them. Those Arabian Bedouins are tails of the Yankee.
Leave them behind, those Arabians;
looters of the same feather flock together.
Their fragile crowns will be consumed by fire.
Let's not bother ourselves, Abul Surra,
with those brittle thrones.
We're on course.
The mud workers expertly led us
out of the valley of darkness
and together we traced the footsteps of the Yankee,

a wild cat from of the Congo jungles
a fennec fox from South America
an Amazon-born crocodile
a Cambodian tiger
and Om Rakhamalla[5] from Mexico.
We gathered under a scorching sun,
and in a single file marched ahead to the Statue,
determined to spit on the eyes
of a free world fattening us for our slaughter day,
Come out! Come out sun.
Show the way to my house.
Our elders have passed.
My shadow is guarding my shadow.

Another important feature this musdār shares with the classical Bedouin musdār, besides the structure and Bedouin spirit, is the employment of dialogue. One notable difference, however, is that dialogue in the classical musdārs is limited to the poet, his sweetheart, his friends, and his camel and is serene in tone, whereas in al-Gaddāl's text it involves a much wider spectrum. Here we see an unusual mix of actors: a close friend, mothers, a sweetheart, lizards, snakes, tilapias, and a huge chorus of other creatures. In contrast to the serene atmosphere of the classical musdārs, compatible with the underlying theme of longing and reminisces, al-Gaddāl's piece comes in a high-pitch tone, which matches the prevalent air of tension. These distinctive aspects work together to create a full-fledged work of drama.

Al-Gaddāl will be remembered for having opened a new path for Sudanese poetry and for taking Bedouin poetry to new levels by establishing it firmly as a medium for creatively rendering some of the themes of modern life. Some of his poems are rendered in urban vernacular Arabic and address diverse themes such as patriotism, inequality, and nation-building. An example of this is the following piece, a symbolic romance poem where the beloved refers to the homeland. Even in this patriotic ambience, the Bedouin images, such as the gazelle and the green plants, are present. The poem was adapted into a popular song by the legendary singer Muṣṭafa Sīd Aḥmad.[6]

How cute is my beloved!
in her amazing dark skin,
the elegant glance of a gazelle!—
and the lush greenness of a *naal* tree,
nestled on the waist of the Nile.
I can't stop singing her praise in verse and prose.
A wildflower whose eyes are soaked with longing for the soil,
whose forehead is glittering with sweat of the poor,
and her mind is occupied with their worries.
She's always worried about me
But never loses her composure
Thanks to her I plucked fear out of my heart.

سمحة وسمرية محبوبتي ولفتاتا غزاله
خضرة ومسقية جنب النيل مشتولة الناله
دا هواك يا بنية كتبتو قصيد وبقولو مقاله
بتفتحي في معاني غناي تديلا مجالا
زهرة وبرية بشوق الأرض عيونا كحالا
تريانة ندية بعرق الناس والناس في بالا
يا خوفا علّي عقل وثبات ماها الولواله
من فرحي البيَ قلعت الخوف وكستني بساله
قت ليها النِيّة متين نتلمّ والحال بطاله
قالتلي غنية وانت معاي
مستورة حاله
بت سودانية محبوبتي ولفتاتا غزاله

Below is the full Arabic text of the "Musdār Abu al-Surra lil Yanki" (Musdār of Abul Surra to the Yankee), along with numbers corresponding to a glossary at the back of the book to help readers understand the local terms.

مسدار أبو السره لليانكى
أمّاتى[1] القبيل بى حِنَّهِن[2] لجَّنٍّـي
گَـرْفَـه وقَـلْـدَه كيف شوق اللبن رَجَّنٍّـي!!
حُزْناً جانِـي فى ميع الصبا يلجِنٍّـي
أطلع منٍّـي يا جلْدى المِنمٍّـل جِنٍّي

وأطلع منى ياحُزْناً بِقى مكجِنِّي[3]
خَلّـنـي ابْدَا مُسْداري
واودى قفاَي لى داراً بِـقَـتْ[4] مي داري
جيتها وجلدى بينو وبين عضاىَ[5] الشحمه
إلا النار بقت قَدامى
جلدى الليله بينو وبين عضاى . . . المافي[6].
إلا ترانى شوَّال الكِـبِـسْ[7]
نفِّيخ جراريب[8] الورم هَـدَّامي[9]
فى جلدى الورم؟ قولن لي . . .
ولا صحي[10] الورم عَـضَّامي؟

سفريتك ما فى النيه
ما ها الكانت مَـحَـريَّـه[11]
خابراك عِـرِّيف
زم العربان ولا قيام الورديه؟
مالك ؟ تريان[12] ومنَـدِّي
كاسي الكِـتّان والهندي
قولَك كِكِّيف ؟!
ترجى البيشان[13]. . . ولا الغربه ال بالزندى؟
برقاً عِـبدِلِّـي[14] الوزنِ
يا طاش . . . يا جاب المزنِ
فرِّقْ ياالضيفْ
فعل الغضبان . . .
أم فرفيرات[15] الحزنِ؟
وشِـن القعده يا ابو السُّـرَّه؟
شن القعده فى ضل العمارات ام كَـمِرتاً[16] بَـرَّه؟
ضُـقْنا الحنضل اليانكي[17]
وبلعنا المره
كملت كوتة التمباك[18] صَـقَـعْـنا الجِـرَّه[19]
وكت إتقفلت شِـقِّيش[20]. . . قَـبَلْ بالمره
نرمي امُرنا فى بلد المعاني الحُره؟
الشم[21] خَـوَّختْ[22]
بَـرَدَنْ ليالى الحرَّه . . .
تلقاها ام خدود الليله مَـرَقَتْ بَـرّه[23]

مرقت بره . . .
تغلى مدِيدة الحِلْبه التسمِّنْ ردفها!!
السمن الـمَـبَـسْـتَرْ . . . يانكي.
والويقود[24] بعيرات الدخان فى العين
وفي الفَشْفَاشْ[25] يسوِّي عمايلو
شن فايدة مديدة الحلبة؟
الويقود . . . وشالو اليانكي.
يا ابو السرة
قامت من دخاخين العمى
تلمّع وشيها[26]
اليانكى مستنيها . . .
كان اليانكى مستنيها فى مراية السَجَم فى الليل
لقيتها متل فريخ الطير.
مرَقْ ود عينها من ود عينها
رجّافة المزمّـلْ حُمّـى، جَـفَلتْ مِنو وقعت عندى . . .
صدرها يغلي . . . يأبو السره شفت اليانكى فى ود عينها.
شلتها للبَحَـر يمكن يغسِّلْ عينها من اليانكي.
فُـتْـنا الحَجْـره[27] بالكَـتَّه[28]
وغطسنا مسافة تبقى قَـدُرْ مسالك الريده،
ما لاقانا من يغبانا، فى البحر الفَـدَرْ تحتانى . . .
ناس عارفاها—ناس عارفاك—ناس عارفاني.
لاقيت القَعُوي[29] والبلطى، قَرقور السمك
ودّاني لى دابي[30]الخُـشَـشْ[31]
نادينا عمال الطمي، الصارقيلة[32]
والقرموط وود المويه . . .
فتنا عليها كانت نايمة، عَجّال[33] البحَـرْ حارساها . . .
كانت نايمه بين حجرين وضُل ساسويه[34].
مسكنا دَرِبْـنا،
عمال الطمي الصحُّوها لـمُّوا حصى البَحَرْ،
قسموه، يات من كان سبِـعْ جـمْرات،
دابي الخُـشَة قال: أدوها فى الجمرات تلات سبعات.
قلنا: أدوها فى الجمرات تلات سبعات.
مسكنا دربنا،
عمال الطمى الصحونا خابرين الدروب،

مَرَقوبْنا في مشرع مسارب الضي،
لقينا الدنيا تترجَّانا قوقى[35] القمرى،
خَوَّى صقير[36] وعوَّى حدَىْ[37]
وعمال الطمى الصحوها لمو على البيعرفوا الصَّيْ[38].
حصى القيزان دوابي الدارقه[39]
والسحليه والناس التحت.
الناس التحت خابرين عمايل اليانكي
مره معونه للغَّاف ومره دوانكي
شِن معناها جبيها اكان ملوه بوانكي[40]
صوتها مكتَّمُه القَرَبيْن[41]،
سيوف وسوانكي.
قولَن للأخلوا ديارُه
دمَّك فّرهد في نارُه
غوَّر في الأرْض، طاروا صقريْن
أولاد الأرْض ما طاروا.
لحمي غطى بن عمِّي
شو صار حالو يا إمِّي
منديل العِرض؟
في بيتِ الدينْ
دمِّي ما يخلِّي دمِّي.
قُمنا من دير ياسينْ
صرنا في جذر التينْ
عم نسقى بعضْ
حُب الزيتونْ
بَدُّو يرجع للطينْ.
صابرا تحت الداوريه؟؟
صابرا فوق الداوريه
يا حال الضد
لحم الطفلين
نابِت غصن الحريه.
جذرى مو في شاتيلا
ما قال حالى ياويلا
حِنَّا في الارض
أرضْ فلسطينْ

يأمى هيلا هيلا
يأمى هيلا هيلا
هيلا وهيلا يأبو السره كُج[42] العينْ
تخَبْـر الشينه من الزينْ
تَـفُـرْز الطاري من الشاري
يأبو السره كج العين
ومدو صباعك السبابي
قول للغافي: يا زول هُوي.
ارخى الغُـرْدَه[43] للعَـنَّافي[44]
شد القِمْري[45] بالحوبابي[46]
فى مسدارنا شلنا نهارنا
يأبو السره
فى إيدينا من ساسُو البَحَر عقدين
مَـسَـكنا دَرِبْـنا
عمال الطمى الصحونا
خابرين الدروب مرقُوبنا[47]
فى مشرع مسارب الضيْ
لقينا الدنيا تتحرانا قوقا القُمرى
خوَّى صقير وعوَّى حديْ
وعمال الطمى الصحونا خابرين الدروب . . .
;وكنا جماعه
دابَّـات الأرِضْ
والسايمه
عوَّامة البَـحَـرْ
والطيرْ
وحتى الغيمه
قَـصَّـاصة الآثر فوق راسنا
شيافه الدَرْبْ
ضنيب[48] اليانكى.
قال القمرى للضُـلِّيله:
-خَـلِّيك صاحيه
زوغ اليانكى لا يودِّرنا
قال الدابي:
-إن يغباها ما يغبانى

ولما الشم[49] مودِّعه غاربه،
وصَّت جُملة الصَّقَّار عيونهم كارْبه
ابقوا ألِفْ بفوت للمِتْلَكُم ناهضين
وفوق ديناب[50] عريباً غادي
قال السحلى:
-لا نغشاهُ
ديل عربان توابع اليانكي.
قال الجمع:
-لا نغشاهُ
ديل عربان توابع اليانكي.
خَلُّوها العريب الغايبه
والسراق طبيقهُ معاهو
تيجاناً عروشها الخِرْوِع[51] الهَشَ العويش
النار تعَلِّب[52] فوق عُقال العرش
ولا خصَّانا بى هدي[53] العروش الهُرْبَة[54]،
يأبو السره، لا عقّال.
مسكنا دربْنا،
عمال الطمى الصحونا خابرين الدروب
مرقوبنا من وادي الضُلُمَّه الكان
عُقُب لمَّينا فى باقي الجَمِع
قاصَّين دريب اليان . . .
سَنُّور الغِيَبْ[55] فى الكنغو
صَبَراً[56] من جنوب أمريكا
من كَلْهاري[57] ديباً ضارى
والتمساح وليد أمازون[58]
ونمراً فى النمور كمبودي
وأم رخم الله[59] مكسيكيه.
ولمَّ لميمنا والشمس البتوقد فوقنا
شدَّ شديدنا لي التمثال[60] مَشَيّل روقنا.[61]
عالَم حُر يدوعِل[62] فوقنا
لى يوم سوقنا[63].
نبصق فيهُ فى عينيهُ جَرْ واسوقنا[64]
يا شمسي طِلِّي طلي
شاوري ع بيتى دِلِّى

كيال الكيلْ؟
ختياري ماتْ
ظِلّـى عمْ يحرس ظلي.
عادل ع خَيِّي مَـيْلي
خَـيِّي ما يحمل شَـيْلي؟
ما خَـفَّ الشَـيْلْ
ثانـي المراتْ
ناطِـر رصاصي سَـيْلي
عَـيْـني فى الفيل . . . ما ظِـلَّه
كِـلْـنا نِـدْريه ما نْضِـلَّه
يا ويل الويلْ
نِـرمي الجَـمْـراتْ
عَدْ المستشهِـد كِـلَّه

12 Al-Ḥārdallo's Poems

Musdār al-Ṣayd

مسدار الصيد

The sun called off its blaze.
Nights traded their simoom for cold breeze.
Lightning filled the sky, sending chills down.
Wings of a darting falcon snapped a tiny bird,
and out of her hiding came the one with charming cheeks.

الشّمْ خوّختْ بَرَدَنْ ليالي الحرّه
والبرّاق برق مِن مِنّا جاب القِرّه
شوف عيني الصقير بي جناحو كَفَت الفِرّه
تلقاها ام خدود الليلة مَرَقَتْ برّه

Expert at choosing their rest and grazing zones,
near branch streams in public they are seen.
Across lush and dry terrain,
all the way from the upper lands they descend.
Meet no harm may they,
to the all-gracious Lord I pray.

تعَرِف لي مشاهد الرُّقاد والفَرّه
فلاّخ المصب بيهو بْتَبين تِتْورّا
فوق حَيَا فوق مَحَلْ من الصعيد مِنْجَرّه
شاحد الله الكريم ما تلقى فيه مضره

Ab-ʿArraaq is in full bloom;
Bashandi flowers lending their fragrance to the air.
At the slightest sound, they [oryxes] shrink in fear,
in high terrain they take shelter.
They should now be around Mount al-Gilaiaa umm Ghurra.

أب عرّاق فتق قَرْنو المِبادر شرّا
الباشَندي عمّتْ مهششيب الدِرّة
من النّقْرة كل حين فوق عِليو منصرة
ها الايام محاريها القليعة ام غُرّة

Their sharp ears from afar picked a thunder.
A heavy mass of clouds showering on Mount Cartut.
Expansive depressions there sometimes held some water.
May my gracious Lord treat them to a good sip this time.

قَدَمَت من هِنا وبي ضانْها سِمْعت كرّة
فوقْ كارتوت شخيتيراً تِخَيِّن خرّ
قلاّتو الوُهاط بي لُشْغه قَبْلو مَحَرّه
يا باسطَ النعمْ تسقيها في ها المرّة

From Mount Grain they slid toward the heights;
wouldn't wait for the downpour in Biyya and Balous.
A yellow streak running down to their thighbones;
their white skirts are just fascinating.

بت المن قرين مَرَقن على الجبّال
في بية وبلوس ما بِرْجن الوَبّال
صُفْراً دِرْعَتِن تِدْلّى لا لْبَهّال
وبُيْضَتْ شاشْ قرابيين تريعً البال

They are already out.
My Lord, always there to respond to every distress call,
I implore You to protect them all,
those short-haired, from every tiny corner gather them.

Not a single one missing.
Every day we come up with a new verse, singing their praise.

مرقن يامجيب لي جُملة السُعّال
شاحدَكْ تجمعِنْ من مَطْبَق الحلاّل
ما ينقُّص حساب الدُّرْج ولَو بي عْجال
ونِحنَ نْجيبْ لَهِنْ في كُلّ يومْ مُنْوالْ

Early morning from Mount Baila,
they slid in one line, self-guided,
their massive bottoms adding to their allure.
The Khor al-Ateesh, a land of gravel and sand any way,
is not a great water reservoir.
Its stock barely lasts for a sunny day.

من بيلا الصباح اسّرْبَقَنْ هُمّال
والدوف فوق حقايبْهن كَتَرْتو جَمال
الخورْ العَطيش بَلَداً عَزَاز ورْمال
ومدروك ماهو مِنْ حَرَّ النّهار بِكَمال

Leaving behind Mount Wad Daoul,
the straight-framed in haste pushed ahead,
through the long series of al-Harba plateaus.
At dawn break they were the first arrivals,
at the pools of Ummat Guroud mountains.
How come creatures of such beauty should end up in snares?

عَقَبَنْ وَدْ دَعُول بِجْرَنْ شَفَاقَة عْدالْ
خَتَمَن مِقْرِح الحربة الْ جبالَ طْوال
قَلْتْ امّات قرودْ وَرَدَنّو بالقُبّال
خِلَقَنْ كيف برمُّولهن دَميرْ حَبّال؟

Taking a north route from Ummat Rimaila series,
to the east they heard thunder crack,
and clouds spreading their heavy cloak,

flashes of lightning wailing out a loud shriek.
Their leader joined them at dawn break.

من امّات رِميلة مْتَرْكِشات لا شْمال
سِمْعَن هَدَري لا قدّام كريزْ واضْلال
اشّرحَطْ بِريقِنْ راحْ إشيلْ وَلْوال
وتيسِنْ زاعَلِنْ باكِرْ مع الشّهْلالْ

Their male leader went about to explore the area,
leaving them behind to graze the *bagail* and *naal*, their favorite meal.
He spotted an overflowing valley.
At Gamzouz some ghosts flickered from the distance.
Around Mount Kaw he found some water.

خلاّهِن رتُوع في بْقيلْ وخَرْجَتْ نالْ
لامَنْ دوَّر الوادي السَّري سيّال
فوقْ قمْزوز طَلَعْ شافْ في مَلينْتو زَوال
وقلْعة كَوْ حفيرْها لقالو فيها نْعال

There they stayed through noon, untroubled.
But once moisture-laden breeze hit their nostrils,
they rose to their feet,
full of longing for their rich pastures of Hagusirwal.
No verse can capture their grace,
no matter how eloquent the poet is.

مِطاّمْناتْ هِناك لامِن نِهارْنْ زالْ
وشَرَفَن كُلَّهِن شمّن دِعاش أتعال
مابْيات البَلَد دايرات حَقُو السَّروال
وصفاً متَّع الغنّاي قَدُرْ ما قال

Though it was the latter part of the day,
they started to prepare for departure.
I can't fill my eyes of their natural beauty,

their dark eyes, untouched by kohl.
After a brief feed on *haweel*, they now feel energetic and fit.
For the likes of me, such a highbred is surely beyond reach.

في عاقِب نِهار سوّنلهن مُرْحال
وعينيهِن خْلَقْهِنْ زُرْقْ بَلا كَحّال
من ريح الحَويل بِقْيَن دحين في حال
وديل ليمْهِن على النّاس ال مِتِلْنا مْحال

He came back just before sunset,
intent on setting off at night,
braving all perils.
Noble mannered, they know no meanness.
Around al-Sirooj they grazed on dry *bigail* grass.

جاهِن مِنقَلِب وقتاً عصير وشَفَاف
وكاسِبْ ليلو بيهِن من صَدَفْ ما بْخاف
ديل ال طَبْعَهِن دايمَ الأبَد عِيّاف
وفي نايط السروج لقيَن بِقيلَن جاف

Toward Mount al-Mazaar, visible from afar,
they sent a leader expert at discovering fresh pasture.
Eschewing Mount Wad Nahar to avoid any possible hunter,
near Sibron he found fresh *bigail* grass.

حَجّار المَزار الْ مِن بعيد بِنْشاف
جرَّن فوقو دورِنْ الْ للقَفُر عراف
لافِخْ وَدْ نِهار من البِحومْ طرّاف
لِقى سِبْرون بِقيلو من المَلينْ موجاف

Over the mountain he saw lightning flicker.
Although pregnant, their steps were not heavy yet.
Through a narrow strait at Snaaf they came out.
Beyond reach of the most powerful, let alone the likes of us.

شاف بَرْقَنْ بِقُلْ فوق الجَبَلْ رفْراف
وهِنْ وحَلْ الدُّرار يا الليلة مِنّو خْفاف
كم عند المضيق مرقنْ هناك بي سناف
ديل قِسْيَن على القوي وال مِتِلنّا ضْعاف

From afar they shine like white birds.
Thin-haired, molded into perfect figure,
no out-jetting shoulders.
Admirers and singers are mouthful of praise,
for their impeccable beauty and perfect grace.

لونِن من بعيد متل البليبلي نْضافْ
حُرْد ومَعَصراتْ من شبّة الاكْتاف
لي النْاس البغنولِنْ يجُرّوا القاف
مالياتْ الخشُم من كامِل الأوصاف

Driven away by mosquitos and flies,
they pushed forth between al-Gisayra and Firai' Gilbus.
At Sadr al-Marma they found a side unpopulated.
After a decent meal of its sparse plants,
with full stomachs they collapsed to rest.

اتنفضَن من الغَبْش اب صِهيب ناموس
وجَن بين القِصَيْرة وبين فِريع قِلْبوس
سَدْر المَرْمي لِقْيَن رِدّو مو مانوس
وطاحَن من حقيقيصو المعيز أرموس

Leaving them in wait at Ḥajar al-Ṣifayyah,
at al-Dahsaraib he found *gombaar* and cucumber vines.
Are these fascinating oryxes any less in charm,
than necks with gold pendants studded?

خلاّهن على حَجر الصِفَيّة خْبوس
ولقى في الدهسريب قُمبار وعِرْق فَقّوس
في المَخلوقة شِن تشْبه مَعيز امْ روسْ
غير ال في وَريدِن شولَقِن مرْصوصْ

Their leader always on the lookout for rich pastures,
always on the run chasing the lightning on the horizon.
So many chasers ended in despair and pain,
as the oryxes outraced their hunting dogs.

تيسِن لي مراتِعهِن تملِّي بْكوس
وديمَ بْقُلْ علِى البرق ال بِشيل حَرْقوص
كم زولاً رقد فوق درْبِهِنْ ممغوس
ومنو اتخلسن ما صَيّدَنْ جاموس

Two males went about exploring the route,
at al-Simair they spotted rich green pasture,
rich dark like Turkish coin, never before trodden.
At a spring with tall reed canes they quenched their thirst.

قامنْ منّهنْ اتنينْ مضاكرَه تْيوسْ
ولِقيَن في السِّمير ختّاً وجيع مَكْبوسْ
دَمَجاً ازّرَقْ مُشْهادو مو مَعَفوص
ورَدَنْ منّو في الميَع المَقامو البوص

There they stayed for two full weeks.
From Odaid I could see their frontline
climbing Mount Gouz Kadies, a cold wind with drizzle greeted them.
That was the outmost post of Buṭāna plains, a safe haven for everyone.

أخدن فيه سِبوع دورين حِسابِن تامْ
من أوديدْ بَزاول شَرْفَهِن قِدّام
طَلَعَنْ قوز كديس جاهِن صِقيط نمْنام
وصْلَن حد بطانَتْ مَركز العُدّام

The Shamal wind presaged the end of rainy season.
Water now only available in depressions.
Only a few days left to delivery and the lying-in month,
those expectant oryxes, in white and yellow like brand textiles,
were back from reed-covered highlands.

الهِنْريمْ طَلَقْ جابَ المَيَع حوّام
من شَهَرْ النُّفاس فَضَلَنْ لَهِن أيّام
انقلَبَنْ من القوز ال مَقامو تمْام
لونِن بِشْبَهْ البَفْتَ الجديدْ والخام

Brisk and robust by nature,
their rest place this time of the year,
is the shade of Wad Ḥārir's acacias.
Soon they will give birth to cute babies, soft and hornless.
For their protection against the evil eye I invoke Quranic verse.[1]

ديل الطبْعَهِن بالْحيل خُفاف وهْمامْ
في سْمِيرْ ودْ حَرِيري مِضَقلّات كلْ عام
قِربن لي مواليد الرّخيصْ وبْعام
ومِن عينْ البِعاين سورة الأنعام

They are now set for departure.
Keep them in your guard, my Lord,
just as you provide cover,
for budding petals and for the sleeping.
In broad leaps, their male leader went west,
looking for a soft terrain for them to give birth.
He came back to a thrilling reception,
as they gaily lined up ready to set off.

نَوّن بالنجيع يا سابلْ الأكمام
أسْبِلْ سِترْك السابِلْ علِى النّيّام
تيسِنْ جَكْ مِغَرّب وبي المَلاين حامْ
جاهِنْ وعافَطَنُّو وحِيل سَدوهنْ قامْ

With the rainy season coming to a close,
they set off from al-Saraweel, leaving behind a wasp-infested place.
Around al-Aashanoug they grazed on some sparse plants.
Their male leader chose a bushy batch to keep them out of sight.
Back by noon he ordered them to embark.

من دَعَتْ السّراويل قبّلن دارتاتْ
علي العاشنوقْ لِقَنْ زوزاي وبي فارّات
عسْكَرْ خافْ عليهِن في ضَرا مَيَعات
وجاهِن زاعلِن بَعَدْ النّهار ما فات

From the east they reached Chabluk from behind the three trees,
passed by Om Suwaibat with its gravel and aromatic *hamaraib*.
For a resting place they spent all night searching.
In the morning around Talhaat they found one.

ختمن"شابْلُكْ "العارْقْ التّلاتْ شَدَرات
ومَرقَنْ فوقْ عَزازْ حَمَرِيبَتْ امْ سوباتْ
داشَن لا الصباحْ ما لقن لَهِنْ مِرْحاتْ
لامَن لِيَّنِنْ باكر علىَ الطّلْحات

Leaving them at al-Furoukh to stay the night,
in a depression at Om Maymoun he saw green plants.
Though scattered over the highland, they looked lined up as if threaded together.
On seeing him back, they merrily ran down to him like falling leaves.

خلاّهِن على رِدْ الفُروخْ بايتاتْ
وفي المكفَى الورَى امْ مَّيمونْ لِقى ختيتاتْ
مِتْماسِك سَدوهِن وبي الحُدوبْ شاتّاتْ
جاهِن وعافَطَنو وجنُو مِنْحتّات

Always shunning populated places,
in highlands taking refuge.
Their male leader scouted the valley behind the mountains.
Proud of his company: slim by nature, not for dearth of food.

ديل الديمَة مِن رِد الانيسْ ناجعاتْ
وكُلْ حِينْ فوقْ عِليوَنْ نابِي مِنْجَمْعات
تيسِن دوّر الوادي الوَرَا القلعات
ضُمّر خِلْقة مو مِن قِل معاش ضايعات

At Damukiyaat he left them behind.
It must be pleasantly cold around the branch streams of Alfaar valley.
In a cluster of trees intercepted by *hamaraib* plants they gathered.
They were due to give birth any time now.

خلاّهن علي رِدّ الدموكيّات
فِلَخْ الفارْ مِسيلباتو اتلَقّنْ بارْدات
قِرْبَن حَضّرن بو ولي النُّفاس دانْيات
وفي دَرْدورْ شِدير ومَعاهُ حَمَرِيباتْ

In the shade of tall reeds they finally gave birth,
breastfed, and wiped hanging fluids off their newborns.
How many solemn, bearded men composed erotic verse,
longing for them, and recalling good old days.

انحَلّنْ جَناهِن في ضَرا نالاتْ
لامن رَضَّعَنُّو وجفْ مِن السّبْيات
كمْ فوقِنْ دِقوناً وَلَّفَنْ قافاتْ
قالن دوبَه ليهنْ والزمان الفاتْ

Praise for their beauty never stopped,
from passed-aways and living alike.
How many before me have admired their dark eyes,
including renowned poet Wad ab-Shawarib.

الحي في الوجود والقالو قَبْلَنا ماتْ
كلّه بْلاهِي بي لَهَجْ الطريفيات
شِن ما قُلنا فوقْ دُغْس العيون ساويْات
قَبْلي ود أب شوارِب جابْلَهن كلْمات

My Lord, who laid out the earth, erected seven heavens,
created all creatures, both barefoot and shod—
against all evils protect those dark-eyed,
until they steer clear of Mount Baila, no one missing.

يا باسطَ الأراضي والسّبِعْ سَمَوَات
وكُلّ الْبدْبي فوقِن حافي واْبْ نعلات
دُغْس العين تنَجّيهنْ من الآفات
لامِن وَخَّرَنْ بِيلا المَعيز جامْعات

Coming out through the buzzing straits of insect-infested Mount al-Khawi,
they slid down the water routes to Abu Raihan valley.
Startled at seeing under the acacia trees what seemed like a figure of a man,
they sought refuge in the nearby mountains after females named.

مَرَقَنْ من مِطِيبْقات الخَوِي اب دُنّان
وهَكَّعَن فوقْ مَعالْقَ الوادي ابو ريحان
شافَن في السِّمير زَوَلَة وحِيامتِ انْسانْ
ونَطَحَنْ ها القِليعْ المَسْمِى بي النّسوان

Expecting to meet some hostile animals at ab-Jarad valley,
their first lines appeared on Qarradh highlands.
Those inhabitants of plains and mounts
are not like the domestic ones,
who offer for slaughtering their young ones, saving their own lives.

الوادي ابْ جراد حَزَرَنُّو بي حَيَوان
وفوقْ الدَّبَّة قَرَّاض شوف شِرِيفِن بان
المِعْزَة المَراتِعن سهول وقْنان
ما انْجَبَدَنْ تَناييهن سَدَاد في سْنان

They slid through the valley straits.
I lost sight of them; like defeated hunting dogs, my eyes retreated in despair.
I sat still, helpless and confused.
Help me catch up with them again my gracious Lord.

وكْتْ ادّرْدَقَنْ بي مَطْبَقْ الوِديان
كلبي الشّارعُو فيهن جا مِنْقلبْ هَقْلان
واتحيرْ قعدْ ساكت بقيتْ مَحَنان
يكتب لَي لِماهِن ربّنا المنان

Exhausted, their male leader came back,
dragging his feet, from a long journey in search of pasture.
They found a flowing stream at Ab Sa'ana valley,
for whose mint he has long been craving.

تيسِن جا من الرحيح ضَبْلان
من قَفُر بلداً بَعيد قَشْيان
اب سَعَنَة الرشيد لِقْينُّو خورو ملان
بثْفلّت علي نعناعو ليهو زمان

At al-Fajkha alone he briskly set off,
made a round behind Ommat Remaila,
and at al-Matna around some fresh grass he regrouped them,
led them past Baila toward Qala' al-Bagar, where they camped.

من الفجخا هَبَرْ خلاّهن
لامن دوَّر اماتْ رِميلة وجاهِن
عند المَتْنَه في عاقباً جديدْ لمَّاهن
ختمن بيلة، فوق قَلَع البَقَر دلاَّهِن

Driving past Mount Wad Daoul,
they were startled at seeing a ghost from afar.
For leading them to grazing places and water their leader took charge.
They reached the mouth of the valley and deep inside took shelter.

قطَعَنْ وَدْ دَعولْ وادَّنْ قِليعو قَفَاهِن
جَفَلَن من زوالْ شوفاً بَعيد باداهن
مَلْزومْ بي مراتِعْهِن وخِبْرةْ ماهنْ
وِصْلَنُّو المصب واتْوكَّرن في ضَراهن.

Living on grass to silence thirst and hunger.
Though over forty in number, no *Ansari* ever took
away any of them.[2]
To sing for them I have permission from mayor Wad al Baseer.
Behold, Zubair, how sweet my tongue turns when I sing their praise.

المِعْزَ البِجازَنِنْ ديمَه فوقْ في خَلاهِن
بالْغات النصاب أنصاري ما زكّاهِن
من ود البصير جايبْ إذن بي غْناهِن
شوفِن يالزبيرْ في لْساني ديل مَحلاهِن

It's not me who would forget them no matter what.
Rain or drought, I never stop composing verse of praise for them.
In tribute of their beauty, son of Zarih[3] and other folks made legendary verse.
From all vermins I implore Saint Sidi al-Hassan to keep them harmless.

مِن عَوَج الوكِتْ ما بَتْركِنْ وانساهِنْ
فوق حَيَا فوق مَحَلْ دايماً بَجُرُّو غْناهِن
ناسْ ابن الذّريخْ ضَرَبو المثل بي جَناهِن
ومِن كل السوام سيدي الحَسن يِبْراهن

Miscellaneous Quatrains

NOSTALGIA

Confirmed news from home: The Buṭāna plains were hit by heavy rain.
Pouring all night long, it continued unabated into the morning.
Male crickets raged with lust; udders, even of young cattle, grew full,
and she-camels enjoyed a lush meal within a short stroll.

الخَبَر اَللكيد قالوا الْبُطانة اتّرَشَّتْ
ساريتنْ تبَقْبِقْ ل الصباح ما انْفَشَّت
هاج فَحَلْ أمْ صِريصر والمنانح بشَّتْ
وبت ام ساق على حَدَب الْفريق اتعشَّتْ

Great news from Aḥmad;
the valley is full to the brim, he said.
I can't see why we should here stay,
with no money to spend,
or a soulmate to drive boredom away.

الخَبَر اَللكيد الليلة أحمد جابو
قال الوادي سال واتْقَرّنَنْ تبّابه
إن سَعَلونا نِحْنَ قْعادنا شِنْ أسبابه
لا مصروف ولا زولَنْ بِنِتْسَلابه

Last night flashes of lightning set the sky ablaze.
Rumbling thunder played havoc with my homesick heart.
A flock of grouse was cruising around the "Hau" water ponds.
Lightning threaded the Buṭāna dwellings into a long embrace.

البارِحْ بشُوف بِشْلَع بريق النَوْ
وحِسْ رعّادو بجْرَح في الضمير گَوْ گَوْ
داك كير القطا دوّر مشارع الهَوْ
وفَرْقان البطانة اتْماسَكَنْ بالضَّو

ROMANCE

Last night I was with her,
soft and green as a cane on a watercourse.
We were chatting and laughing, and hours flew by.
Until ostriches fell off horsebacks
in the race to the sky's exit gate,
she was not responsive enough,
but was not entirely tough.

البارِحْ أنا وقَصَبة مَدَالق السيل
في ونسة وْبَسِطْ لامِنْ قَسَمنا الليل
وقْتين النّعام اشّقْلَبَن بُو الْخيل
لا جادتْ ولا بِخْلَتْ علَي بالْحيل

Among her age or older, she's peerless
If ʿIbdillah and the folks could see her,
and the necklace over her ample chest dangling,
they'd excuse my absence from their Eid gathering.

الزول الصّباه فاتْ الكبار والقدْرو
كان شافوهو ناسْ عبد الله كانوا يعذْروا
السببْ الحماني العيدْ هِناكَ أحَضْروا
دُرْديق الشّبيكي الفصّلو فوقْ سدْرو

The likes of Ḥamdiyah never ride on donkey back.
She never gives you a satiating drink.
When in a generous mood, she would only give you a small sip,
leaving you desperate for more.

حمْدية السِرور ما ركّبوك فوقْ عَرْ
ما بتمجِّدك تقْطَعْ قَراك بالمرْ
إن جادتْ عليك تدّيك مِويخراً دَرْ
وعُقبان ترْبِعَكْ لامن تضوق الشَرْ

In vain I tried to contain my longing for al-Tayah.
It's turning painful like snakebites.
When I recall her curled hair and glittering earrings,
My passion for [Um Na'im] is as strong as ever.

غَيْ التابة دَسّيتو وأبَى يندسْ
أوّل كان ملاسِعْني وْدحين بانْ بسْ
تِحتَ العُقْلة وقْتْ اتلامع الگسْگسْ
قدْر النملة مِنْ غَي أم نعيم ما خسْ

The white-necked oryx around Ellao al-Ni'am mound often seen
has shackled my mind to the glittering beads on her hair.
Her spear, naturally sharp, needs no further grinding,
from close range penetrated me.

دَرْعاتاُ على عليوّ النَعام مراقه
دَرَجَتْ عقلي فِي نجيم عُقْلَته أم براقه
تَفْ أم إيد نَفِجْ حَرْبَتَه مي زرّاقه
حادة برا نَفِخْ فوراً كتير وطراقه

O creator of the universe
I have been holding a big secret deep in my heart,
unwilling to share it except with one who can appreciate it.
The young oryx at the heart of the green valley,
has been playing havoc with my heart, folding and unfolding it.

يا خالق الوجود أنا قلبي كاتِمْ سِرُّو
ما لقيت مِنْ يدرِك المَعْنى بيهو أبِرُّو
بَهَمَتْ مَنْصَح الوادي المِخَدَّرْ دِرُّو
قَعَدَتْ قلبي تطوي وكل ساعه تفِرّو

The most proud among mothers of girls is by all means Neela,
who gave birth to one with legs cast to perfect measurement and a slender figure.
If I had an affair with her,
I would never think of any other woman—Arab or else.

في امات البنات حايداني ولدت نِيله
وساقاً دَقّوْ صبْ عُقُبْ القناية عديله
أنا وايّاها كان بيناتنا جارية خليله
اقنع بيها مِن غَيْ العرب والعيله

Last night rumors almost split us apart.
But proven false, the fun did start.
Dancing like a cane on the stream mouth,
the stripes on her cheeks have owned my heart.

البارِحْ حَديسْ الناس بِدُور افْرِقْنا
كُلُّو مرَقْ كِضِبْ عُقْبان صِفينا وْرُقْنا
الدرعة أم شلوخاً سِتةّ مالكة عشُقْنا
تتمايخْ مِتِلْ قَصَبة مَناصح الحُقْنه

HEARTBREAK

Repent her love, friends urged me.
But how can I forsake one,
with such a neck, long and proud?
Of me her passion wouldn't let go,
beyond cure, like a mystic lover I grew.
Don't think even Prophet Job as much pain endured.

إتلموا الجماعة وقالوا لِيّ تتوب
من العُنقو زيّ الشمعدان مصْبوب
فاتْ فِيّ الفوات وبقيتَ زي مجذوبْ
الحاس بيهو ما ظنيتو مسّ ايوبْ

Heartache's put its marks on me, visible to all.
My very life is now at stake.
If I ever get to have a deep inhale from her armpits,
nothing will ever put us apart again.

غيّها فيّ ظاهر للبدور معرِفْتو
في الباين علي دمّي العزيز انا خفتو
عرقاً في المناكبْ كان كِتِبْ كارفتو
داك لومَكْ علَيْ ما تقول عُقُبْ فارقتو

Heavy worries landed on me.
Distracted and distant all day and night;
a gaunt tummy with a bruised heart I turned.
Even solid stones won't stand such pain.
Yet I never lose hope in the Lord's blessing.

كَبَس الْهَمْ علَيْ ليلي ونهاري مْسرّحْ
بطني اشّيمَطَتْ قلبي البِفِر مِجّرّح
الصايدني كان صاد الحُجار بِتْمرّح
لكنْ رحمة المولى الوسيعة تْفَرّحْ

Newly sustained wounds
left me upset, whimpering, and sleepless.
In my pain of longing for the naturally dark eyes,
Laila's lover is better off—at least he gets some slumber.

ظهرنْ فيّ ها الأيام جِروحَه جْداد
بتكَدّر وانوح والنوم عَلَيْ ما عاد
مِنْ فَرْقْ أمْ دُغُسْتاً خِلقة مي مُرْوادْ
معَشوق لَيْلَى أخيرْ ما لايَ ضاقلو رْقاد

I yearned for the time when I was my own master.
Riding long distances to reach them [my girlfriends].
To their lips I was expert at finding my way.
That was a time when life was particularly nice to me.

كم شويَمْ لِهنْ وكتاً بفاقِقْ ورَيّس
كمْ ودّيت لِهن من عِندي واحدْ كَيّس
بسْرِقْ دغْمَتِنْ نَعَمِنّي فيهِن سَيِّسْ
دا وكتْ الزمان بِلْحيل مَعانا كويّسْ

On a palm frond bed and a straw mat, I spent a sleepless night.
My shed hardly offering any shield from cold and rain.
Kept awake by memories of her sweet coquettish whisper till dawn,
I couldn't get up in time to load sorghum on camel backs.

البارِحْ رُقادي گَسيدة فوقَه بْريش
راكوبةً تجيبْ صَقْطة وْمعاها رّشيشْ
اللحماني ما اشهّل جُمال العيشْ
هُنْهيناً بِسوّنّو الدّغش بي شيشْ

Mount Wad Diyab is still inhabited with oryxes.
Their young jubilantly playing around.
Should I with the means be endowed,
I would forsake my own home and choose theirs as my abode.

قوزْ ود ضياب يا اللّيل تَرَى بي شْياهو
بَهَماً بِطَرِّدْ فرحان وعاجبو خلاهو
زولاً في ام قدود المولى كان أداهو
بِقْعُدْ عِنْدَهِنْ بِتْرْك لَهِنْ ماواهو

Can't you see where I ended up?
One day unconscious, another an aimless wanderer.
I can't stand my parting from a soft sweetheart,
who bears resemblance to the Basyai oryx.

ما بتشوفني هسّع بقيت مي ياي
يوماً تبْ أغيّبْ ويوم أطشْ بي خلاي
فَرْقْ النية بلحيل قلْ عليّ حياي
فيها شبه خِلَق بُرِّيبة الباسياي

My longing for this young oryx who left Dirrat al-Karrami,
left me a gaunt figure with weak bones.
My passion for cheek-striped al-Tayah gave me sleeplessness.
She has all the beauty features of a young hornless oryx.

من ديفةَ الْ بغادرَنْ دِرّت الكَرّامي
اللحم انْسَلَبْ رابَنْ عليّ عضامي
التاية ام شليخ حسرورها قلّ منامي
فيها مَكَمَّلات خِلق الجدي البعّامي

Sick of longing for a smile beaming from afar, like glittering clouds.
Aimlessly wandering under the hot sun.
Al-Tayah's beauty is comparable to none,
except mountain-dwelling oryxes.
But to be honest, O 'Amāra, I'm also attracted to al-Sarra.

الفِرّه البرا المِزْرَى اب سحابةَ جارّه
شِنْ درّعني العيا ولَفْح السُّواجه الحارّه
شبه (التايه) في شات القَنانه الفارّه
لا كين يا عماره قلبي رايد (السارّه)

My verse is tasteless without a good mention of Gazira.
My village Reira is thrilled to host such a beauty.
Soft thighs and a cushioned breast,
and a necklace like a white streak on a young oryx.

بلاش غنانا الما ذكَّرنا جَزيره
نار بيها البلد واتشرفتْ بَهَا ريره
ليِّن فخدَها المِتْل المَخَدَّة سْديره
فيها شويرة اللدتو أمه محيره

THE ORDEAL

Gone is my herd of cattle that'd suck many wells dry.
Today for handfuls of sorghum I sold ab-Nāmah, my cherished sword.
Truly, life can be tame enough to be led by a spider's thread.
But can also be stubborn enough to break free from steel reins.

بعد اَمْ بوح تقطّٖطْ جامَت لْلعداد
بِعْت "اب نامه" بِي قِيمَتْ عَشَرتْ امداد
إنْ جادتْ بِي خيت العنكبوت تِنْقاد
وان عاقتْ تقطّٖع سِلسِل الحدّاد

Today I feel like one who went on a no-return trip,
or one whose arrow went too wide.
Like braids of hair swinging in a woman's neck,
our fate is swinging in the hands of our Creator,
who alone can decide when to take our souls back.

الليله علي مِثْل ألْ خَتَرْ ما عاد
والليله علَيْ مِثْل أل زَرَقْ ما صَاد
اليوم يا امْ وَريدنْ نفّض اللُباّد
ترى الراس بقْطعُه الخالِق مِتين ماراد

Even the sons of Ḥamad, once the resort for everyone in need,
have now left, crossed the Atbarawi River to Abyssinia.
Their women with thick hair in oil soaked
are in tears for leaving Reira and their company behind.

رحلوا أولادْ حَمَدْ ألْ للبلَد رُكّازَه
قَطَعوا الأتْبَراوي منوّيين بالبازه
ستات اللَكيك ألْ عقْلَتِنْ نزّازه
بِنْكّن بالدموع لى ريره لى من حازَه

Look around, 'Abdallah.
You will see young oryxes,

tottering around in rags.
What a grieving loss is ab-Sa'ad, folks.

يا عبد الله خوي أنظر قَدُر ما كان
ما شُفْتَ البَهيم الصيد جَنَى الجِذْيان
دجّنْ بلِّرِضْ كسُّوهِنْ الدُلْقانْ
واوجعي الشديد رَقَدْ أبْ سَعَدْ ياخوانْ

Go to the towns, ʻAbdallah, and see for yourself,
the girls of Matamma, their hair disheveled,
water skins on their shoulders—
and instead of hair oil and oily perfumes,
lice rampaging through their heads.

يا عبد الله خوي أغْشَ البنادر شوفِنْ
بَنّوت المتمّه اجّدَلَنْ صَفُّوفِنْ
شايلات القِرَبْ والسعون في كتوفِنْ
وبعد خُمْرَه ودِهان سال القَمُلْ برْفُوفِنْ

FAREWELL

The heavenly camels have arrived,
like a flock of pigeons lined up on the horizon.
Time to leave a world from which, alas, nobleness and modesty are gone.
But I'll always miss my beloved valley, ever bountiful and green.

زمْل القدرة جَنْ وفي الوَطا ما خَتّنْ
طارن لى السماء وْمِثْل القماري اسّتّنْ
الجُود والحَياَ منّ العِقول انختّنْ
طال الشوق على الوادي ابْ عِيوشَنْ شتّنْ

Arabic Glossary of Local Terms

	LOCAL NAME	MEANING
1	أماتى	أمهاتي
2	حِنَّهِن	حنانهن
3	مكجِـنِّي	كاره لي
4	بِـقَتْ	صارت
5	عضاىَ	عظامي
6	المافي	اللاشئ
7	الكِـبِـسْ	جوال لترحيل القطن يكبس فيه كبساً
8	جراريب	جمع جراب
9	هَـدَّامي	جمع هدمة – ثوب
10	صحي	صحيح
11	الكانت محرية	التي كانت مرجوة
12	تريان	مفعم باللين
13	البيشان	جمع البوش- الاحتفال
14	عِـبدِلِّـي	من جهة القبلة، ويقال أيضاً عبّادي
15	فرفيرات	واحدها فرفرة
16	كَـمِرتاً	كاميرا التصوير
17	اليانكي	الأمريكي
18	التمباك	التبغ
19	صَـقَعْـنا الجِـرَّه	أصلها عماية الاجترار، وهي هنا مستخدمة مجازاً للإشارة إلى اضطرار الشاعر لاستخدام التمباك (النشوق الذي يوضع داخل الشفة السفلى ثم يبصق) عدة مرات لعدم توفر مخزون كافٍ منه.
20	شِـقَّيش	من كل جهة
21	الشم	الشمس
22	خَـوَّختْ	مالت وضعفت حرارتها

23	تلقاها ام خدود الليله مَرَقَتْ بَرّه	جزء من بيت شعر للشاعر الحاردلو الكبير شاعر البطانة
24	الويقود	الوقود
25	الفَشْفَاشْ	الرئة
26	وشيها	وجهها
27	الحَجْره	الشاطئ عالي الجرف
28	بالگـتّه	السباحة بالصدر
29	القَعُوي	الضفدع
30	دابي	الثعبان - المقصود هنا التمساح
31	الخُشَـشْ	الأعشاب والشجيرات الكثيفة على الشاطئ تكون موطناً للتماسيح
32	الصارقيلة	دود الطمي
33	عَجَّال	عجول
34	ساسويه	الحجر الصغير الأملس
35	قوقى	غنّى
36	صقير	تصغير صقر
37	حدَىْ	حداءة - نوع من الصقور
38	الصَّيْ	القفر
39	الدارقه	الثعبان أبو درق - الكوبرا
40	بوانكي	بنكنوت - فلوس
41	القَـرَبـيْنْ	السلاح الناري
42	كُج	ركز نظرك
43	الغُـرْدَه	حبل يحزم به البعير
44	للعَـنَّافي	نوع من أنواع الجمال في السودان، قوي وسريع
45	القِمْري	أسم الجمل
46	بالحوبابي	حبل
47	مرقُوبنا	مرقوا بنا
48	ضنيب	تصغير ضنب - ذنب/ذيل
49	الشم	الشمس
50	ديناب	بيت الأعراب
51	الخِـرْوِع	نبات ضعيف الساق
52	تعَـلِّـب	تشتعل
53	هدي	هذه
54	الـهُـرْبَـة	المنهارة
55	الغِـيَـبْ	جمع غابة
56	صَبَراً	حيوان الصبرة
57	كَـلْهاري	صحراء في الجنوب الأفريقي

58	أمازون	نهر في أمريكا الجنوبية
59	أم رخم الله	صقر ابيض ضخم بطيء الحركة والطيران
60	التمثال	تمثال الحرية في أمريكا
61	مَـشَـيِّل روقنا	الجمع يسير في خط واحد
62	يدوعِـل	يسمن
63	يوم سوقنا	يوم ذبحنا
64	واسوقنا	آلة يجر بها التراب لتسوية الأرض - زراعة

Note: Local terms are identified by number in “Musdār Abu al-Surra lil Yanki” in chapter 11.

Notes

INTRODUCTION

1. *Ramya*, in Arabic, which literally means a "thrown piece," is sometimes performed as a song of its own, but more often is rendered as an introduction to a longer song.
2. Al-Wathiq, "Awzan al-Dobait al-Sudani," in *Majallat Majma'a al-Lugha al-Arabiyya* [Arabic language academy's journal], 138–39. See also Ibrāhīm and ʻAbdin, *al-Ḥārdallo, Shā'ir al-Buṭāna*, 21.
3. Al-Wathiq, "Awzan al-Dobait al-Sudani," 139.
4. Al-Ṭayyib, *al-Dobay: Dirasa an Buhur al-Ghina' al-Sha'abi*, 17–19.
5. Al-Ṭayyib, *al-Dobay: Dirasa an Buhur al-Ghina' al-Sha'abi*, 39.
6. *Fadag* is a Beja word meaning "four"; hence, her face like is a fourteen-day moon (ten plus four).
7. Babikir, *Modern Sudanese Poetry*, xxviii–xxix.
8. While cattle usually produce milk only after they have given birth, young ones who are yet to give birth can produce milk when the rainy season is particularly prolific, giving birth to rich pasture.

1. AL-ḤĀRDALLO'S TIME

1. Al-Ḥārdallo, *Diwan al-Ḥārdallo*, 3
2. Ibrāhīm and ʻAbdin, *al-Ḥārdallo, Shā'ir al-Buṭāna*, 14.
3. *Mitairig* is the diminutive, or colloquial, form of *muṭrag*.
4. Al-Ashraf refers to people from the family of Imam Al Mahdi; al-Ashraf literally means "people of noble origin."
5. Ibrāhīm and ʻAbdin, *al-Ḥārdallo, Shā'ir al-Buṭāna*, 14.
6. Ibrāhīm and ʻAbdin, *al-Ḥārdallo, Shā'ir al-Buṭāna*, 14.
7. Ibrāhīm and ʻAbdin, *al-Ḥārdallo, Shā'ir al-Buṭāna*, 14.
8. Ibrāhīm and ʻAbdin, *al-Ḥārdallo, Shā'ir al-Buṭāna*, 14.
9. Ibrāhīm and ʻAbdin, *al-Ḥārdallo, Shā'ir al-Buṭāna*, 14.
10. Ibrāhīm and ʻAbdin, *al-Ḥārdallo, Shā'ir al-Buṭāna*, 14.
11. Ibrāhīm and ʻAbdin, *al-Ḥārdallo, Shā'ir al-Buṭāna*, 14.

12. Ibrāhīm and ʿAbdin, *al-Ḥārdallo, Shāʾir al-Buṭāna*, 14.
13. Ibrāhīm and ʿAbdin, *al-Ḥārdallo, Shāʾir al-Buṭāna*, 14.
14. Al-Ḥārdallo, *Diwan al-Ḥārdallo*.
15. Ibrāhīm and ʿAbdin, *al-Ḥārdallo, Shaiʾr al-Buṭāna*.
16. Ibrāhīm and ʿAbdin, *al-Ḥārdallo, Shaiʾr al-Buṭāna*.

2. ROMANCE

1. Horne, *Ancient Arabia*, 5:19–40.
2. Al-Muttalibi, "A Critical Study of the Poetry of Dhu' r-Rumma."
3. Horne, *Ancient Arabia*, 5:19–40.
4. Salah Ahmed Ibrāhīm (1933–93) was a prominent Sudanese writer, poet, and diplomat. A graduate of the University of Khartoum, he taught at the Institute of African Studies at the University of Ghana from 1965 to 1966 and later served as Sudan's ambassador in several stations. His collections include *The Ebony Forest*, *The Rage of the Hebaba'y*, and *Death and Us*. Salah's poetry is replete with references to Greek mythology, Islam, and to Arabic and African cultures. He was an outspoken opponent to all forms of suppression and lived up to his principles until the very last day of his life. In the early 1970s, he resigned his diplomatic post as Sudan's ambassador to Algeria in protest against the execution of Communist Party leaders and took political asylum in Paris, where he led an austere life as freelance writer. In *Death and Us*, a tribute to his family members whom death had snatched one after the other, Salah extends an open invitation to death to feel free to come whenever it "craved for more."
5. Muḥammad al-Mahdi al-Majzoub (1919–82) was born in al-Damar, northern Sudan, to a renowned Sufi family. He graduated from the School of Accountancy at Gordon Memorial College (now the University of Khartoum). Al-Majzoub was a transgenerational poet who tackled virtually all forms of poetry, from the classical to *taf'ila* all the way to prose poetry. He left behind ten collections of poetry.
6. From "Wedding Parade," in Babikir, *Modern Sudanese Poetry*, 2–4
7. The Qurayshis and Tamims are two prominent Arab tribes. Muhammad el-Mahdi el-Majzoub, "Intilaq" [Freedom] in *Nar al-Majazeeb* (Khartoum: Dar al-Jeel Publishing, 1982) from the introduction to Babikir, *Modern Sudanese Poetry*, xv.
8. Muhammad el-Mahdi el-Majzoub, "Fajrun Kathoob" [False dawn] in *Nar al-Majazeeb* from the introduction to Babikir, *Modern Sudanese Poetry*, xv.
9. Introduction to Babikir, *Modern Sudanese Poetry*, xiv.
10. El-Khatim, *Muraja'at fil Thaqafa al-Sudaniyyah*.
11. This tradition of the celebrative whipping of young males as part of wedding festivals, which dates back to the early nineteenth century, is largely associated with the communities along the Nile Bank. It developed out of the conscious need to

instill courage and endurance in the hearts of young generations to prepare them for defending their tribe against external threat. It eventually developed into a source of pride, a social value, and a tradition associated with marriage festivities.

The line—Tonight, mother of the bride, we brought you, our cream of the cream—is rephrased from the following song, which girls sing once the bridegroom's parade approaches the bride's house:

أم العريس جينا ليكي جبنا العريس باركناه ليكي

12. See Ibrāhīm, *al-Afro Arabiyya aw Tahaluf al-Haribin*, "Afro-Arabism or the Coalition of the Escapists," *Majallat al-mostaqbal al-Arabi* [Arabic future magazine] 2, no. 2, 1987.
13. Madani, al-Amin Ali, poet and critic (1900–1926), was an outspoken critic of traditional poets and one of the early advocates of literature inspired by the local setting. His articles, which were first published in *al-Hadara* newspaper, later appeared in book form under the title *A'raas wa Ma'atim* [Festive and morning times] one year after his death. See al-Fiya, *fi al-Adab al-Sudani* [Sudanese Literature], 10–11.
14. "Cheek striped" means beauty facial marks.

3. THE NATURE LOVER

1. *Ab-'Arraaq* is a veiny plant.
2. Ibn Zarih (son of Zarih) is a seventh-century Arabic poet, nicknamed Majnoun Lubna, or the "mad lover of Lubna."

4. AL-ḤĀRDALLO'S STYLE

1. Khalid Fathal Rahman's interview with Tayeb Salih, Sudan TV, https://youtu.be/_lih0L69aei.
2. "On the Poetry of William Wordsworth," Poet Seers, accessed December 13, 2020, https://www.poetseers.org/the-romantics/william-wordsworth/library-2/poetry-william-wordsworth/.
3. Samuel Hamilton, "The Characteristics of Keats' Poetry," *Seattle Post-Intelligencer*, December 13, 2020, https://education.seattlepi.com/characteristics-keats-poetry-5145.html; "Nature," CrossRef-It.Info, December 13, 2020, https://crossref-it.info/textguide/john-keats-selected-poems/40/3048.
4. John Keats, "Ode to a Grecian Urn," Poetry Foundation, accessed December 13, 2020, https://www.poetryfoundation.org/poems/44477/ode-on-a-grecian-urn.

5. THE MUSDĀR

1. Hureiz, *Fan al-Musdār*.
2. Hureiz, *Fan al-Musdār*, 24–27. Aḥmad 'Awad al-Karīm Abu-Sin was born in 1908 in Reira, in the heart of Buṭāna, where he spent a good part of his childhood and

adulthood before settling in Khashm al-Girba to lead a sedentary life as a farmer. He was a prolific poet with six musdārs and numerous marbū'‘s to his name. ‘Abdallah Ḥamad Wad Shawrāni was born in Buṭāna to al-Marghūmab tribe. He composed several musdārs, which reflected a deep knowledge of the stars. Al-Ṣādiq Ḥamad al-Ḥallāl (wad Āmna) was born in al-Sifayyah in Buṭāna, and, like Aḥmad Abu-Sin, he settled in Khashm al-Girba but continued to use his camel in all his travels between various cities. Al-‘Āgib wad Mūsa was born in Buṭāna. He composed two musdārs and countless marbū‘.

3. Ḥureiz, *Fan al-Musdār*, 13
4. Ḥureiz, *Fan al-Musdār*, 14
5. Ḥureiz, *Fan al-Musdār*, 21. The Bedouins have their own ways of monitoring weather conditions and the change of seasons. Each of the four seasons is divided into seven *‘inas* (represented by stars with locally designated names). Each star, or *‘ina*, lasts for approximately thirteen days and is associated with a certain part of the season. In the above example, the disappearance of al-Naṭiḥ star indicates that temperature is set to soar.
6. Ḥureiz, *Fan al-Musdār*, 22
7. Ḥureiz, *Fan al-Musdār*.
8. Ḥureiz, *Fan al-Musdār*, 16.
9. *Greyhound* is a reference to how fast his camel can run.
10. Ḥureiz, *Fan al-Musdār*, 18.
11. Ḥureiz, *Fan al-Musdār*, 19. *Tiyatro*, Latin for "theater," was commonly used in Khartoum in the early twentieth century. It was introduced by Europeans who lived and ran business in Sudan at that time. Tiyatro Khawaja Louiso was a famous entertainment center in Khartoum at the time. The reference to the word in the above quatrain is allegorical, however, alluding to sensual moments.
12. Ḥureiz, *Fan al-Musdār*, 18–19.

6. MUSDĀR AL-NIJUM

1. Ḥureiz, *Fan al-Musdār*.
2. Barrati is a high quality brand of jewelry.

7. MUSDĀR RUFĀ'A

1. Ḥureiz, *Fan al-Musdār*.
2. A pet name for his camel, al-Gomri literally means "turtle dove," a reference to his speed.
3. *Annafi* is a camel of pure descent.
4. *Kaharaib* is a camel of modest breed.
5. Ḥureiz, *Fan al-Musdār*, 19.

6. A pet name for his camel.
7. Mihairt al-Khail means the "princess of horses," referring to his sweetheart.

8. THE ROLE OF BEDOUIN POETRY

1. Muḥammad al-Wāthiq, *al-Shi'r al-Sudani fi al-Qarn al-Ishrin*, 17
2. Reads "Black" Sultanate, in line with the traditional Sudanese convention of referring to black as blue.
3. Muḥammad al-Wāthiq, *al-Shi'r al-Sudani fi al-Qarn al-Ishrin*, 6–7.
4. Muḥammad al-Wāthiq, *al-Shi'r al-Sudani fi al-Qarn al-Ishrin*, 10–11.
5. "Huruf Ismik," was written by Hashim Siddig (b. 1957), a poet, playwright, critic, and journalist. He earned a BA in criticism from the Music and Theatre Higher Institute in Khartoum in 1974 and did further studies at the School of Acting in Essex, United Kingdom. He wrote more than ten poetry collections and scores of plays for radio, TV, and theater.

9. THE BEDOUIN POEM

1. *Bashir* is the bearer of good tidings, in reference to Prophet Muḥammad.

10. THE MUSDĀR AND THE ḤAQĪBA

1. Ibrāhīm al-ʿAbbādi is a prominent poet, born in Omdurman in 1894. A dobait poet, he was instrumental in the transformation from dobait-intensive lyrics to the *ḥaqība* song. He was also a playwright and a pioneer in dramatic poetry.
2. *Mushra'a* is a drinking point for animals.
3. Muḥammad Aḥmad Sarour, a famous Sudanese singer, was an instrumental figure in the transformation to the ḥaqība era. A friend of the poet, he was the one driving the Fiat on this trip.

11. CONTEMPORARY MUSDĀRS

1. Muḥammad Ṭāha al-Gaddāl (1951–2021) was a prominent Sudanese folk poet and activist whose colloquial poems are rich in local reference.
2. For more on the Sabra and Shatila massacres, see "The Dispersal of the PLO from Lebanon," Britannica, https://www.britannica.com/place/Palestine/International-recognition#ref479036.
3. Abu al-Surra is a friend of al-Gaddāl's.
4. These are the opening lines of al-Ḥārdallo's "Musdār al-Ṣayd."
5. Om Rakhamalla is a scavenger eagle.
6. Muṣṭafa Sīd Aḥmad (1953–96) was a popular Sudanese singer and musician, with more than a hundred songs to his name. Many of his songs express the longing for freedom and the struggle of the Sudanese people against dictatorship.

12. AL-ḤĀRDALLO'S POEMS

1. The original refers specifically to Quran's chapter al-'Ana'am (Cattle).
2. I believe he means to say that unlike the domestic cattle, which are subject to taxation, those oryxes are beyond the reach of local authorities, the Ansar (those loyal to the Mahdist), many of whom serve as tax leviers.
3. Ibn Zarih (son of Zarih) was a seventh-century Arabic poet nicknamed Majnoun Lubna, or the "mad lover of Lubna."

Bibliography

Babikir, Adil. *Modern Sudanese Poetry: An Anthology*. Lincoln: University of Nebraska Press, 2019.

Dahab, Ṣalāḥ. "Al-Ḥārdallo fi Qaṣidatihi al-Malḥamiyyah Musdār al-Ṣayd." *Al-Khartoum* newspaper, February 10–13, 2000.

Fathal Rahman, Khalid. Interview with Tayeb Salih, Sudan TV. https://youtu.be/_lih0L69aEI.

Fiya, A. A. al-. *Fi al-Adab al-Sudani* [Sudanese literature]. Damascus: Ninawa Publishing, 2011.

Ḥārdallo, Ibrāhīm al-. *Diwan al-Ḥārdallo*, 5th ed. Khartoum: al-Dar al-Sudaniya Lil Kutub, 1991.

Horne, Charles F., ed. *Ancient Arabia*. Vol. 5 of *The Sacred Books and Early Literature of the East*. New York: Parke, Austin & Lipscomb, 1917.

Ḥureiz, Sayed Hamid. *Fan al-Musdār*. Khartoum: Khartoum University Press, 1976.

Ibrāhīm, al-Mubārak, and ʿAbd al-Majid ʿAbdin. *Al-Ḥārdallo, Shā'ir al-Buṭāna*. Khartoum: Al Tamaddon Printing Press, 1957.

Ismā'īl, ʻIzz al-Din. *Al-Shi'r al-Qawmi fi al-Sūdān*. Beirut: Dar al-Awdah, 1968.

Khatim, Abdel Goddous el-. *Muraja'at fil Thaqfa al-Sudaniyyah* [Reflections on Sudanese culture]. Omdurman: Abdel Karim Mirghani Cultural Centre.

Muttalibi, ʻAbd ul Jabbar Yusuf al-. "A Critical Study of the Poetry of Dhu' r-Rumma." PhD diss. SOAS University of London. DOI: https://doi.org/10.25501/SOAS.00028993.

Nasrallah, Muḥammad Ridha. Interview with Tayeb Salih, MBC Satellite Channel. https://youtu.be/Yx9yvKsSA-A.

Ṭayyib, al-Ṭayyib Muḥammad al-. *Al-Dobay: Dirasa an Buhur al-Ghina' al-Sha'abi* [The Dobay: A study of the forms of folk poetry]. Omdurman: Mohammad Omer Bashir Center for Sudanese Studies, Omdurman Ahliya University, 2002.

Wāthiq, al-. "Awzan al-Dobait al-Sudani." *Majallat Majma'a al-Lugha al-Arabiyya* [Arabic language academy's journal], 4th ed. (2000): 137–56.

Wāthiq, Muḥammad al-. *Al-Shi'r al-Sudani fi al-Qarn al-Ishrin, Ara'a wa Qasaid Mukhtara*. Khartoum: Khartoum University Press, 2009.

Index

Ab-'Arraaq (plant), 40, 50, 108, 135n1
'Abbādi, Ibrāhīm al-, 90, 137n1
'Abbasi, Muḥammad Sa'id al-, 78, 79
'Ābdīn, 'Abdul Majid, 3
'Abdullahi, Calipha, 12, 14, 15, 77
ab-Jarad valley, 117
ab-Nāmah, 16, 127
ab-Sa'ad, 128
ab-Shawarib, Wad, 43, 116
ab-Tiboub valley, 71
Abu Raihan valley, 117
Abu-Ṣalāḥ, Ṣālih 'Abd al-Sīd, 83, 85, 86
Abu-Sin, 'Abdallah, 13, 55, 56, 58, 59, 60
Abu-Sin, Aḥmad, 11
Abu-Sin, Aḥmad 'Awad al-Karīm, 8, 56, 57, 58, 59, 90, 135n2
'Amāra Abu Sin, 15
Amīn, Muḥammad al-, 19, 80–81
angaraibs, 82
annafi, 71, 136n3
Ansari, 119
Arabian Peninsula, 6, 55, 76
Ateesh, Khor al-, 109
ayatib, 4

Badīnah, 70
bagail, 41, 110
bahama, 54
Baila, Mount, 44, 51, 109, 116, 118
Balaib, al-, 69
Balous, 40, 108
Bāngair, al-, 61
Banna, 'Umar al-, 78
Bashandi (flowers), 40, 50, 108
Bashīr, al-Tijāni Yūsuf, 78
Baṣīr, Wad al-, 15, 16
Basyai oryx, 125
Batāhīn (tribe), 77
Beja, 3, 4, 76
Bitain, al- (place), 47
Biṭain, al- (star), 62, 63
Biyya, 40, 108
Buṭāna, 4, 6, 7, 8, 9, 11, 12, 18, 22, 38, 39, 45, 48, 49, 61, 62, 69, 76, 77, 78, 96, 113, 120
Buthaynah, 22

Cartut, Mount, 40, 50, 108
Coleridge, Samuel Taylor, 5

Dabarān, al- (star), 62, 64
Dabbat al-Aasaad, 72
Dahsaraib, al-, 36, 46, 112
daifa, 54
dalluka, 30, 34
Damukiyaat, 43, 116
dar'aa, 54
Darfur, 78, 79

Dhalma, al-, 73
Dhul-Rumma, 5, 8
dilka, 33, 34
Dirrat al-Karrami, 36, 125
dobait, 2, 3, 52, 77, 81, 82
dobay, 2, 3, 52
Ḍurā', *al-* (star), 62, 65

Ellao al-Ni'am, 36, 53, 122

fadag, 3, 4, 133n6
Fan al-Musdār (Ḥureiz), 55
Farrāsh, Ibrāhīm al-, 55
Firai' Gilbus, 112
Funj (Islamic State), 76
Furoukh, al-, 42, 115
fussaib, 54

Gaddāl, Muḥammad Ṭāha al-, 8, 94, 96, 99, 137n1
Gamzouz, 41, 110
garmaṣiṣ, 33, 34
Gedaref, 5
ghuna, 2, 3
Gilaiaa umm Ghurra, Mount al-, 40, 50, 108
Gilaila, 47
Gisayra, al-, 112
gombaar, 36, 46, 112
Gomri, al-, 70, 72, 73, 74, 75, 136n2
Gouz Kadies, Mount, 113
Gouz Rajab, 56
Grain, Mount, 40, 108

Hagusirwal, 41, 110
Ḥajar al-Ṣifayyah, 36, 46, 112
Hak'ah, al- (star), 62, 64
Ḥallāl, al-Ṣādiq Ḥamad al- (wad Āmna), 56, 135–36n2
hamaraib, 43, 71, 115, 116
Ḥamdiyah, 22, 37, 121
Han'ah, al- (star), 62, 64
ḥaqība (lyric song), 8, 53, 79, 83, 90, 95
Ḥārdallo, al-, 1, 2, 3, 4, 6, 7, 8, 9, 11, 12, 13, 14, 15, 16, 17, 18, 19, 20, 21, 22, 24, 25, 34, 35, 37, 38, 39, 44, 45, 46, 47, 48, 49, 50, 51, 52, 53, 54, 55, 61, 75, 96, 107, 113, 120
Ḥārdallo, Ibrāhīm al-, 44
Hashim Siddig, 137n5
Hassan, Saint Sidi al-, 44, 52, 119
haweel, 42, 111
Hunda, 90, 91
Ḥureiz, Sayed Hamid, 55

'Ibdillah, 2, 12, 27, 121
Ibrāhīm, Ṣalāḥ Aḥmad, 27, 78
'inas, 62, 64, 65, 66, 68, 136n5
'Itayyid, 61
'Iwah, al- (star), 65, 67

Ja'aliyīn (tribe), 77
Jabhah, al- (star), 65, 66
Jabra, 56
Jamīl of Buthayna, 8, 22
Jamū'iya (tribe), 77
jarrāri (song rhythm), 79
Jazīrah, 35
Juhaynah (tribe), 76

Kābli, 'Abd al-Karīm al-, 1, 2, 4, 18, 19
kaharaib, 71, 136n4
Karim, Muḥammad Aḥmad 'Awad al-. *See* Ḥārdallo, al-
karkaar, 33, 34
Kasala, 69
Kaw, Mount, 41, 110
Keats, John, 5, 7, 47, 48
Khajījah, 22
khalwa, 30, 78

Khartoum, 1, 4, 5, 11, 30, 82
Khatim, Abdel Goddous el-, 34
Khayrasān, al- (star), 65, 66, 67
Kināna, 76
Kitchener, 77
kitir, 72
Kordofan, 78, 79

lakhlukha, 54
Latīf, Ali 'Abd al-, 77
Layla, 22
Luqman, Saint, 87
luttaib, 54

Madani, al-Amīn Ali, 35, 135n13
madīḥ (Sufi songs), 83
Mahdi, Muḥammad Aḥmad al-, 12, 82
Mahdist revolution, 77
Mahdist rule, 12, 17, 77
Māḥi, Hāj al-, 83
Maḥjūb, Muḥammad Aḥmad, 78
Majzoub, Muḥammad al-Mahdi al-, 29, 34–35, 78, 134n5
Mak Nimir, al-, 77
marbū', 2, 3, 4, 7, 45
marisa, 33, 34
Matamma, 14, 128
Matna, al-, 118
Mazaar, Mount al-, 111
Mecca, 83
Mellit, 78
Mihairt al-Khail, 75, 137n7
Mirghaniyah (Sufi order), 69
mitairig, 12, 133n3
mi'za, 54
mu'allaqa, 20
Mubārak, Mount, 57, 90
Muḥammad (Prophet), 83
muraba', 2, 3, 45
Mūsa, al-'Āgib wad, 56, 135–36n2
musdār, 6, 7, 8, 9, 12, 39, 44, 45, 48, 52, 55, 56, 57, 58, 60, 61, 62, 63, 66, 68, 69, 75, 90, 93, 94, 100, 107
"Musdār Abu al-Surra lil Yanki" (al-Gaddāl), 94–99, 100–106
"Musdār al-Mitairig" (al-Ḥārdallo), 12
"Musdār al-Nijūm" (Wad Shawrāni), 57, 62–68, 69
"Musdār al-Ṣayd" (al-Ḥārdallo), 8, 39–44, 45–53, 61, 96, 107–19
"Musdār al-Ṣobagh" (Abu-Sin), 57, 58–59
"Musdār of Gouz Rajab" (al-Ḥallāl), 56
"Musdār Rufā'a" (Abu-Sin), 56, 57–58, 59–60, 69–75
"Musdār Setit" (Abu-Sin), 56, 57, 60–61
mushra'a, 92, 137n2

naal, 41, 100, 110
namim, 2, 3
namm, 2, 3
Naṭiḥ, al- (star), 57, 62, 136n5
Natrah, al- (star), 65
Neela, 122
Nubia, 34, 76

Odaid, 113
Omdurman, 14, 82
Ommat Ragareeg, 71
Om Rakhamalla, 99, 137n5
oryx, 7, 8, 13, 19, 23, 24, 35, 36, 39, 40, 41, 42, 43, 44, 45, 46, 47, 48, 49, 50, 52, 53–54, 56, 61, 65, 67, 70, 73, 84, 85, 91, 96, 108, 112, 113, 114, 122, 125, 126, 127

Pasha, Muḥammad Ali, 77
Prophet Muḥammad, 83

Qarradh, 117
Qays, 8, 22
Qays, Imru' al-, 5, 8, 20, 21

Rabīʾah (tribe), 3, 76
ratina, 83
rayhouba, 54
Reira, 11, 13, 35, 126, 127
Rufāʾa al-Rubba, 69

Sabra and Shatila massacre, 94
Sadr al-Marma, 112
Saint Hasan, 72
sakhla, 54
Ṣaliḥ, Aḥmad Muḥammad, 78
Salih, Tayeb, 46, 47
Salṭana al-Zarqa, al-, 76
Sammaniyah Sufi Order, 78
Saraweel, al-, 114
Ṣarfah, al- (star), 65, 67
Sarour, Muḥammad Aḥmad, 92, 137n3
Sarraf, al-, 70
Sayyāl, 70
Setit, River, 5, 15
shambani, 3, 4
shatam, 1, 18
Sheikh Aḥmad al-Ṭayyib, 78
Shobra valley, 56
Shukriyah (tribe), 5, 11, 12, 15, 56
Sibron, 111
Sīd Aḥmad, Muṣṭafa, 99, 137n6
Simair, al-, 113
Simāk, al- (star), 65, 68
Sinja, 90
Snaaf, 111
Sudan, 3, 4, 6, 8, 9, 11, 12, 14, 17, 18, 19, 27, 29, 33, 37, 46, 53, 55, 76, 77, 78, 79, 80, 82, 83, 90, 134
Sufism, 77, 78
Surra, Abu al- (Abul), 96–98, 137n3

Tāka, Mount al-, 69, 70
Taktūk, Sheikh Faraḥ wad, 76
Tambal, Hamza al-Malik, 35
ṭanābra (sing. *ṭanbāri*), 82, 83
Ṭarfah, al- (star), 65, 66
Tayah, al-, 22, 23, 35–36, 122, 125, 126
Ṭayyib, ʿAbdalla al-, 76, 78
Ṭayyib, al-Ṭayyib Muḥammad al-, 3, 4
Ṭayyib, Sheikh Aḥmad al-, 78
Tirayya, al- (star), 62, 63
Turco-Egyptian administration, 17, 77, 82
Turkish rule, 11, 55, 77

Umayyad period, 8
Um Girain, 22
Ummat Guroud mountains, 41, 109
Ummat Rimaila, 41, 109
Um Na'im, 3–4, 22, 122
Um Rishaim, 22
Um Wad'a, 73
ʿUnaizah, 20

Wad al Baseer, 118
Wad Daoul, Mount, 41, 109, 118
Wad Diyab, Mount, 24, 48, 125
Wad Habbuba, 77
Wad Ḥārir, 19, 43, 114
Wad Mūsa, 71
Wad Nahar, Mount, 111
Wad Shawrāni, ʿAbdallah Ḥamad, 8, 56, 57, 62, 66, 69, 75, 135–36n2
Wāthiq, Muḥammad al-, 3, 8, 76, 77, 78, 79
Wordsworth, William, 5, 7, 47

Yankee, 94, 96, 97, 98, 100

Zainab, 22
Zarih, Ibn, 44, 52, 119, 135n2, 138n3
"Zawarq al-Alḥan" (al-Amīn), 81

IN THE ON AFRICAN POETRY SERIES

The Beauty Hunters: Sudanese Bedouin Poetry, Evolution and Impact
Adil Babikir

www.ingramcontent.com/pod-product-compliance
Lightning Source LLC
Chambersburg PA
CBHW020417230426
43663CB00007BA/1209
* 9 7 8 1 4 9 6 2 3 5 2 0 6 *